Mittel
EUROPA

To Niuta Slesin Titus and
in memory of Beno Slesin;
Stephen, Wendy, Renée and
Danielle Cliff;
Gisèle and Jacques Rozensztroch;
Catherine de Chabaneix

Published by Clarkson N. Potter, Inc., 201 East 50th
Street, New York, New York 10022. Member of the
Crown Publishing Group.

Random House, Inc. New York, Toronto, London,
Sydney, Auckland

CLARKSON N. POTTER, POTTER, and colophon are
trademarks of Clarkson N. Potter, Inc.

Manufactured in China

Library of Congress
Cataloging-in-Publication Data
Slesin, Suzanne.
   Mittel Europa: rediscovering the style and design of
Central Europe / Suzanne Slesin, Stafford Cliff, Daniel
Rozensztroch; photographs by Gilles de Chabeneix.
   Includes index.
   1. Architecture— Central Europe.
2. Architecture, Modern—Central Europe.
3. Interior architecture—Central Europe.
4. Interior decoration—Central Europe.
5. Vernacular architecture—Central Europe.
I. Cliff, Stafford.
II. Rozensztroch, Daniel.   III. Title.
NA954.S64   1994
728'.0943—dc20
93-30142
CIP

ISBN 0-517-58803-X

10 9 8 7 6 5 4 3 2 1

First Edition

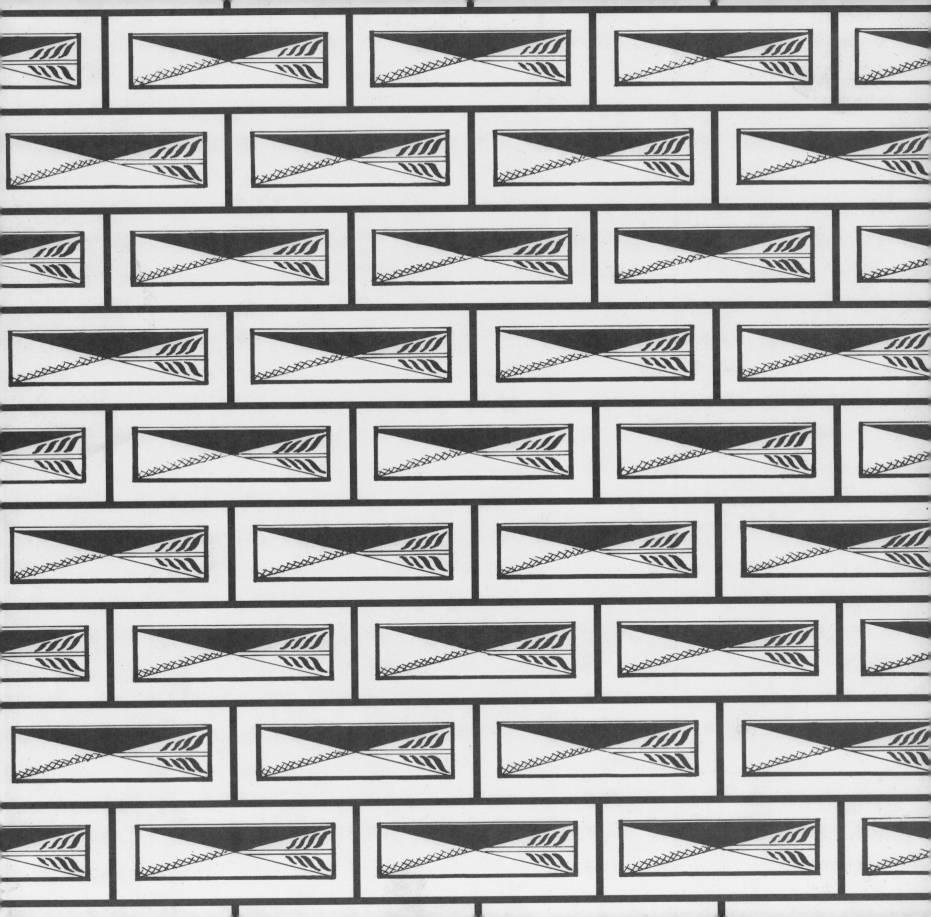

Mittel EUROPA

REDISCOVERING THE STYLE AND DESIGN OF CENTRAL EUROPE

SUZANNE SLESIN

STAFFORD CLIFF

DANIEL ROZENSZTROCH

PHOTOGRAPHS BY
GILLES DE CHABANEIX

DESIGN BY STAFFORD CLIFF
ART ASSOCIATE, IAN HAMMOND

CLARKSON POTTER/PUBLISHERS
NEW YORK

ACKNOWLEDGMENTS

We could not have been able to rediscover Mittel Europa alone. We are grateful to have been guided by many people whom we consider members of our international family.

Thank you Lazare Rozensztroch for defining the perimeters and parameters of Mittel Europa.

Thank you tour leaders, researchers, and patient translators, including Zuzana Evrard Bosnansky in Prague as well as in the villages of Slovakia and Bohemia; Ingrid Zerunian and Susan Pisarkiewicz in Vienna; Lukas Praun in Salzburg and beyond; and Paola Navone, Claudio Mayer, and Viviana de Grisogono in Trieste.

Thank you to all those who opened their homes to us, gave us leads, shared our enthusiasm for Mittel Europa, and supported us along the way. They include Michael H. Adams, Marion Adler, Paul Asenbaum, Julie Bader, Eva Bajczar, Ferenc Bodor, Zita Borszeki, Martin de Chabaneix, Simon de Chabaneix, Ellen Chesler, Viviane Chokas, Susan Costello, Sandor Csepregi, Mary Curtis, Philip Cutler, Maria Dajka, Stephen Drucker, Alice Eisen, Luc and Emil Evrard, Larry Fabian, Adam Farkas, Ferenc Farkas, Aline Fouquet, Mario Franzi, Barry Friedman, Dr. Sepp-Rainer Graupe, Manfred Grubinger of the Salzburger Freilichtmuseum, James L. Greenfield, Ching Guazon, Dr. Istvan Gyorffy, Ian Hammond, Anne-Marie Harrington, Irmgard Hauer-Kochert, Elizabeth Williams Herz, Dr. Ralph Herz, Taria Herz, Arlene Hirst, Michael Huey, Marta Kelemen, Walter Klement, director for North America at the Austrian National Tourist Office in New York, Lore Korbei, Ildiko Korody, Szabo Laszlo, Alan Lindenfeld, Matthew Mallow, Agnes Molnar, Geraldine Mucha, Maria Nagy, Sofia Parrenas, Susan Penzner, Zsuzsa Pereli, Anna-Lülja Praun, Clarice Praun, Isabel Quartin-Bastos, Peter Reimholz, Lesli Rice, Marina Schmutzer, Jonathan Scott, Saija Singer, Louis Slesin, Michael, Jake and Lucie Steinberg, Carol Southern, Wolfgang Steininger, Elisabeth Gräfin Strachwitz, Elisabeth Sukosd, Eva and Iván Tejkalova, Barbara Toll, Hubertus and Huberta Trauttenberg, Marilyn J. White, Gabriella Wiedermann, Selma Wiener, Françoise Winter, and Christian Witt-Dörring.

Thank you to the editors at Elle Decoration and Marie-Claire Maison, in Paris; to Heather Ramsdell, the editor-at-large of the "Mittel Europa Gazette"; and our agents, Lucy Kroll and Barbara Hogenson.

We are grateful for the help and support from our publisher, Clarkson Potter—including Crown's publisher Michelle Sidrane and Potter's editorial director Lauren Shakely, Howard Klein, Esther Sam, Leyla Morrissey, Jim Walsh, and Joan Denman—but especially to our editor extraordinaire, Roy Finamore. Without him, *Mittel Europa* would be simply far less than we hope it is. Thank you all.

CONTENTS

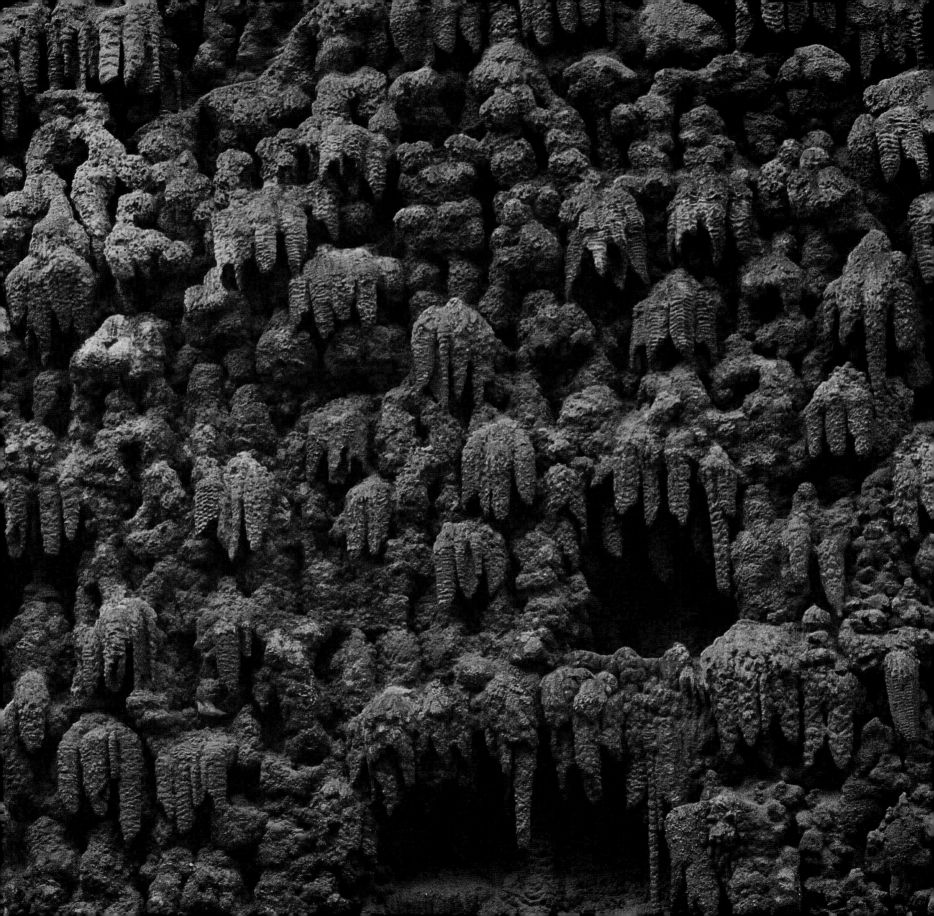

DOORS VIENNA

DOORS PRAGUE

DOORS SALZBURG

DOORS SALZBURG

DOORS PRAGUE

DOORS SALZBURG

DOORS SALZBURG

DOORS HUNGARY

STONE CHURCHES

FOLK ART

MOVIE MOMENTS

FACES

FACES

DECORATION
PAINTED CEILINGS

GROTTOES

DECORATION
CERAMIC STAIR

WOODEN HOUSES

AUSTRIAN MOUNTAINS

INTRODUCTION

STOVES

By the time we had begun to think about doing a book on Mittel Europa, we had already traveled the Caribbean, Japan, Greece, Spain, and New York State in our quest for Style. Mittel Europa seemed to suit us particularly well, perhaps because its boundaries were both vague and yet well defined. Mittel Europa was real; but it didn't exist in its original context anymore. That made it all the more intriguing for us. We chose to explore the countries that were once part of the Austro-Hungarian Empire, that were on the route along the meandering Danube, the large centers and small villages that stretched from Vienna to Trieste.

We decided not to pay attention to political boundaries. Even so, little did we know at the time we began to be interested in the area that its frontiers were about to change radically once again.

The formation of the Austro-Hungarian Empire under the Hapsburgs in 1867 brought together people from vastly different cultures and endowed them with a common history. While political changes and nationalistic ideas would, over time, drastically change that unity, there remained in the daily life of many of these disparate people, and in their art, architecture, and customs, a certain homogeneity of values. One might even be tempted to call it a civilization. It is that civilization of Mittel Europa that we sought to rediscover in the flamboyant Baroque style of the Empire, in the boldness of the emergent and powerful bourgeoisie, in the revolutionary and passionate art and design movements that were to define the first decades of the 20th century.

Most of all we became fascinated with what the writer Stefan Zweig called "the world of yesterday"—the evocative phrase that became the title of his autobiography and described the years before World War I, when he was growing up. Looking back to that more innocent time, Zweig wrote: "Today, now that the great storm has long since smashed it, we finally know that that world of security was naught but a castle of dreams."

Growing up in New York and France after World War II, we were sheltered physically but emotionally aware of the disruptions that inexorably changed and eventually shattered the lives of our grandparents and great-grandparents. We felt that with the world remaking itself once again—with the fall of Communism and the new Europe—it was an especially appropriate time to search for our roots.

Our journey to Mittel Europa began with Daniel's first visit to Budapest and Hungary in 1990. How did the weight of the intellectually and industrially sophisticated Jewish bourgeoisie affect the evolution of what was once the focus of Europe? What happened when this world began to fall apart? What was left for us to experience, to relive? We felt a curiosity, a need to know, a desire to find what remained and to try to perceive how that world had continued to influence us.

We expanded our voyages to Vienna and Prague, the cities—with Budapest—that were to be the reigning trilogy of Mittel Europa. We found many similarities in these three sisters: picturesque neighborhoods with old shops, houses, and churches intact; the inextinguishable remains of the Jewish ghettos, one of the most powerful legacies of all time; and the heady mix of architectural styles that we came face-to-face with at every corner.

We came to realize that what we knew of these places had come to us through art, architecture, music, and design: Gustav Klimt and the Wiener Werkstätte, Joseph Emanuel Fischer von Erlach and Otto Wagner, Wolfgang Amadeus Mozart and Gustav Mahler. We needed the context of the towns and villages, the marble and gilt halls, the well-endowed sitting rooms and the rural farmhouses where life revolved around the stove, to bring it all alive.

Our quest was more instinctive than encyclopedic, based more on emotion than history. Ray Monk, in his biography *Ludwig Wittgenstein: The Duty of Genius*, writes: "The fascination of *fin de siècle* Vienna for the present day lies in the fact that its tensions prefigure those that have dominated the history of Europe during the twentieth century. From these tensions sprang many of the intellectual and cultural movements that have shaped that history. . . . In almost every field of human thought and activity, the new was emerging from the old, the twentieth century from the nineteenth."

Overall we felt more in tune with the modest than the palatial. We were also able to see the ebb and flow of stylistic tastes. In the case of the Jugendstil and Wiener Werkstätte movements we went beyond the appreciation of objects per se. Putting things in their context made them come alive in a more meaningful way.

Always, we went in search of tradition and authenticity. In Budapest, for example, while many buildings are diminished, most of the past is there. Only in Vienna has the intrusion of late-20th-century design left a jarring scar. Once unleashed, change comes quickly. Prague is now in ferment. We felt protective toward this ancient city, so full of nostalgic charm. We felt like saying, yes, you can touch her, fix her up, but please be gentle.

In a grand bourgeois house in Trieste, where the suites of rooms look as if their inhabitants had just stepped outside for a breath of air only to return momentarily, we were as drawn to the less formal rooms as we were to the lavishly decorated reception rooms. In the huge and now quiet kitchen, we could not resist running our fingers over the thick and smooth white marble tabletops or admiring the butter-hued lacquered walls.

But it was in the countryside, in the rural areas of Austria and Hungary, to be sure, but especially in the villages of Slovakia and Bohemia, that we found time had stood still. The buildings, the colors, the furnishings, and most surprisingly the people themselves look much as they did 100 years ago. It is as if nothing in the world beyond—no wars or revolutions—had taken place to change these now old people's lives. We still had the privilege to look into their homes, to discover the pride and beauty of their folk art traditions, and to realize how deeply we love and respond to these things today. We are their last witnesses. When they disappear, it will all be over, forever.

As we rapidly approach the 21st century, the definition of what is new seems to be an important concern. The new unfolds from the old, and the past helps us turn the corner into the future.

In so doing, we allow ourselves to be introspective. And this renewal has become the ultimate gift of our travels. We hope it will prove inspirational for you as well.

Suzanne Slesin
Daniel Rozensztroch   *June 1993*

Three Cities

Vienna, Prague, Budapest. A trilogy of cities. Three sisters whose histories overlapped for centuries and who grew to become friendly rivals in their cultural and political prominence in Mittel Europa. Although close in temperament, each retained its distinctive personality.

At the turn of the century they were at their most desirable. Vienna—the intellectual one—pioneered the modernist movement in all the arts. Prague—the lovely one—dazzled her admirers with the many-hued richness of her architecture. Budapest—with her dual personality—was the most secret and mysterious. Today, in spite of all the turmoils that have touched these three capitals, they survive. They may be old ladies now, but they have not forgotten their youth. On the following pages is a patchwork of impressions of the three cities toward which all of Mittel Europa and eventually the world gravitated.

A marriage of architecture and narrative mosaic in Budapest.

Vienna—the oldest city to be settled on the Danube—was considered the last stop in the West for those traveling eastward from Paris to Istanbul on the luxuriously appointed Orient Express.

Vienna is about civilization, culture, heritage. If the expansion of the Baroque style at the end of the 17th century and the first half of the 18th century reflected the imperial power of the Hapsburgs, then the extraordinary intellectual and artistic bloom that centered on the city at the turn of the 20th century marked the end of the Austro-Hungarian Empire.

Vienna grew from a central core in a number of concentric circles that culminated in the monumental Ringstrasse, the boulevard on which are deployed the museums, the parliament, the opera. But if the city presents a panoply of design styles, it is the work of one, Otto Wagner, that has given Vienna its place in modern architectural history.

For the city's railway, Wagner designed 36 stations, some of which are used today for the subway. And the architect's two apartment buildings on the Linke Wienzeile are among the best of the Jugendstil buildings that defined Vienna's version of art nouveau.

Elegant shops—with the necessary branches in Prague and Karlsbad—opened to serve the needs of a new consumer society. The fashionable Rudolf Scheer & Söhne, shoemaker, bootery, and saddlery, *right*, is still outfitted with furniture designed by Josef Hoffmann for the Gebrüder Thonet company.

The huge aviary in the park of Schönbrunn dates from 1750 to 1775, when the garden was redesigned in the French manner by Adrian van Steckhoven and Ferdinand von Hohenberg. Included on the grounds that adjoin the Schönbrunn Palace are a romantic Roman ruin, the extravagant Palmenhaus, or Palm House, the Gloriette, a neoclassical belvedere, and a zoo, opened in 1752, where the Viennese, under Joseph II, saw a giraffe for the first time.

Otto Wagner's mark on Vienna includes the 1894 Karlsplatz station, top row center—a masterful marriage of art, technology, and design—as well as the 1899 Majolica House on the Linke Wienzeile, a Jugendstil masterpiece, top row left. *The much-loved Saint Stephen cathedral,* middle row center, *with its Romanesque facade and Gothic choir, is the spiritual center of the city. Its construction began in the 13th century; its polychrome roof was commissioned at the end of the 15th century by Matthias Corvinus, king of Hungary. The city is dotted with old stores that still retain their original fittings and can be discovered on main streets or tucked away in small alleys. Old ornamental trade signs hang overhead, and a painted metal shutter or decorative iron grille add to the visually variegated texture of the town.*

Prague has been at the crossroads of Europe for centuries. Ringed by hills, through which meanders the River Vltava (Moldau, in German), Prague has inspired many writers and musicians, including the famous 19th-century Czech composer Bedrich Smetana, who celebrated the city in his evocative symphony *Ma Vlast* (My Country).

Both geographically and culturally, Prague has been sensitive to all the religious, political, and artistic influences that developed around her. The city resulted from five towns that no longer exist independently but today make up its three distinctive neighborhoods. Hradcany and the *Stare Mesto* (Old Town) is an area of charming medieval character, its rows of pastel-hued buildings forming the backdrop to an imaginary operetta. Mala Strana is a village at the foot of the castle, with its dramatic Charles Bridge that for 500 years was the only link across the Vltava. The *Nove Mesto* (New Town) was rebuilt in the 18th century.

The Jewish ghetto, named Josefov in honor of the Emperor Joseph II at the end of the 18th century, is a unique memorial to the Jewish population that first came to Prague during the 10th century as free merchants. By the beginning of the 13th century, the center of life for Prague Jews had shifted to the *Stare Mesto*, where the Prague ghetto was established. At the turn of the century when Prague was restructured, only the Town Hall, six synagogues, and the cemetery remained.

The Grand Hotel Europa, by Bedrich Bendelmayer and Alois Dryak in 1903, is one of the most prestigious monuments of the Secession movement in Prague. Its café, with its oval gallery, *right*, is intact.

With the exception of a few fragments of 14th-century tombstones, the Old-New synagogue is the oldest monument in the ghetto and the oldest synagogue still standing in Central Europe. The old Jewish cemetery in the Josefov dates from the 15th century; people were buried there until 1789. The number of graves is far greater than the 12,000 headstones that can be seen. As time went by, bodies were stacked one atop the other because of the lack of space. The result is a chaotic and injured landscape that cannot help but elicit a powerful emotional response.

Prague's architectural heritage includes the picturesque Golden Lane, a medieval row of tiny houses where the alchemists at the court of Rudolf II experimented in turning base metal into gold and where Franz Kafka would come to write in number 22, top row left; the Town Hall in the ghetto, top row center, first built in a Renaissance style in 1586 and transformed by Josef Schlesinger in 1756 in the Baroque style. The building is adorned with two clocks, one with Roman, the other with Hebrew, numbers. There are many examples of Jugendstil, the decorative style inspired by organic and floral shapes, as in the tile-lined stairwell of the Grand Hotel Europa, bottom row right.

Italian sgraffito with figurative or geometric motifs decorates facades throughout the city, while the many painted, metal, stone, or wood cartouches and signs—which illustrated the occupant's social rank or profession— that surmount the portals facilitated the identification of the buildings before numbers were introduced in 1770. One of the most famous is the House of the Blue Fox, bottom row left.

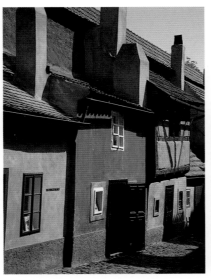

udapest. Buda and Pest—one on each side of the Danube River, bluer and wider than in Vienna. Buda above on the hill, an 18th-century Baroque town with its royal palace, its private mansions, stuccoed in the pastel colors of Italy, interior courtyards, and small winding streets. Pest below on the plain, with its long avenues including the Népköztársaság útja, the pride of the bourgeoisie at the end of the 19th century—lined with the architect Miklos Ybl's impressive apartment buildings, his 1884 Opera House, and the numerous cafés, including the legendary Drechsler.

Budapest, Vienna's rival, the animated Magyar of Mittel Europa, is still seductive after 50 years of physical destruction. Time has nevertheless left her with some magnificent fragments of her past.

The 19th-century Tolbuchin Central Market is at the foot of the Liberty Bridge, designed by Samuel Pécs, *right*, where still today farmers come to sell their fruits and vegetables, including the many peppers that will be used to make paprika.

FRISSEN
TISZTÍTOTT
BURGONYA
ÁLLANDÓAN
KAPHATÓ.

Bouquets of daffodils and tulips sold on the street provide a colorful and cheerful note. Along with the flower sellers who proffer bouquets of violets when the theaters let out, the reappearance of a number of street vendors can be read as a symbol that the once gracious Old World feeling of Budapest is not lost.

Budapest offers a range of styles from the nearly rustic Hungarian Baroque to the strict Bauhaus esthetic. Some of the landmarks that are considered Budapest institutions include the Matthias Church in which the kings of Hungary were crowned, *top row center.* Under the Turks, it became the main mosque of the city until the Franciscans and later the Jesuits transformed it in the Baroque style. The ever popular Széchenyi Baths, the largest in Europe, *bottom row center,* with its elaborate medicinal baths and open-air swimming, encapsulates Budapest's centuries-long involvement with water. The pleasant old Gerbeaud pastry shop, *top row right, is* one of the city's most famous meeting places.

The Aristocratic Style

GROTTOES

With its exaggerated forms and splendiferous details, the Baroque celebrated the spiritual by expressing itself with material means. In the 17th and 18th centuries, in such towns as Prague, Vienna, and Salzburg, a number of aristocratic patrons under the influence of the Italians and the French commissioned a coterie of the most esteemed foreign architects to build the lavish city palaces and impressive country estates and hunting lodges. Painting, sculpture, and architecture came together in buildings that raised the status of Vienna and Prague to the level of the other European capitals.

GROTTOES

But with the events of the 19th century—wars, uprisings, and revolutions—the aristocracy lost some of its powers. This was a period of isolation and retrenchment. The glories of the Baroque period gave way to the more academic and austere building styles of the neoclassical and neo-Gothic.

Today many old families of noble descent struggle to keep their heritage alive. A handful of people live in only a few of the dozens of rooms that were once alive with activities and entertainments.

But sometimes there is a young generation ready and enthusiastic about participating in their family's history. And opening up these grand homes to the public is another way of keeping them alive. The rich ornamentation, spatial grandeur, and quality of execution are the true witnesses of an age when art and architecture were the highest expressions of creativity.

A hunting castle in the Austrian countryside.

Family Seat

ABOVE *At the center of the house is a grand skylit hall with cement tiles.*

ABOVE RIGHT *The wide staircase with its cast-iron railing leads to the second-floor gallery. The portrait that hangs in the dimly lit hall is of a family ancestor.*

The Villa Lanna, in the small Austrian town of Gmunden on Lake Traun, was built in 1871 by Adalbert Lanna. His great-grandson Hubertus Trauttenberg was born in the house and now lives there year-round with his wife, Huberta, and their children. But for his parents, who lived in Prague, Villa Lanna was only a summer residence.

Few things have changed since the house was built. Even today, some of the rooms have no electricity. And the gas chandeliers, which have not been used for decades, are only now being refitted. Although the rooms in Villa Lanna have taken on the patina of age, they have retained a certain vitality and spirit due to the continued efforts of those who live there and protect the house's history.

LEFT AND ABOVE *The study on the second floor is also used as a family sitting room. The mix of furniture was accumulated over time. It includes an armoire and several chests of marquetry. The wing chair has been upholstered with an antique tapestry. The walls have been papered in a dark gray leaf pattern.*

The formal dining room is on the ground floor and is rarely used nowadays. With its huge oval table and 18 tooled-leather-upholstered chairs, it hasn't changed in more than 125 years. The scenic hand-painted wallpaper with its neoclassical themes was the height of fashion when the house was built. The two identical marble and brass fireplaces in the room are set across from each other. The unusual pediments over the doors are also neoclassical in style.

ABOVE *The ceiling in one of the small sitting rooms was painted with clouds and putti. The chandelier was only recently electrified. The electrical wire can be seen strung across the ceiling, as if echoing the cracks in the painting.*

ABOVE RIGHT AND RIGHT *The billiard room, with its dark-paneled walls and green ceramic fireplace, is also the library.*

Hunting was a favorite pastime in the area surrounding Lake Traun, as evidenced by the rows of antlers around the painting of a stag and the stuffed birds that hang below the picture frame.

Baroque Titans

The Baroque style played itself out in all the major cities of Mittel Europa, but especially in Prague. In the first half of the 18th century, Czech architects, as well as German and Italian ones, contributed to making Prague the Baroque capital of Europe.

The style also developed brilliantly in Vienna, but a bit later. The first stage of the Baroque in Austria saw the reinterpretation of the Italian vocabulary, particularly in churches. Then, after many existing palaces were expanded, the Baroque style culminated, after the Ottoman defeat of 1683, with the Hapsburgs, in the Imperial Baroque style.

Among the Italian architects busy working in Vienna was Domenico Martinelli, who conceived the Lichtenstein Palace, with its majestic symmetrical facade. But it was two German architects who brought the Viennese Baroque style to its apotheosis: Johann Bernhard Fischer von Erlach and Johann Lucas von Hildebrandt, both of whom were well versed with the Italian style. One of their masterpieces was the Winter Palace of Prince Eugene of Savoy, a spectacular urban palace that boasts a monumental staircase lined with sculpted figures of Atlas.

Palace facades—such as the Caprara-Geymüller Palace built around 1698, or the early-18th-century Daun-Kinsky Palace in Vienna, or the 1713 Clam-Gallas Palace in Prague, designed by Fischer von Erlach—were enhanced with impressive entrances and lofty portals often framed with pilasters depicting variations on the form of Atlas, usually in exaggerated poses.

Private Palace

I n the mid-19th century, Pasquale Revoltella—a rich banker from Trieste and one of the financial backers of the Suez Canal—commissioned the German architect Georg Heinrich Friedrich Hitzig to build a palace that would display Revoltella's collections of paintings and sculptures.

A majestic marble staircase, long galleries, and large rooms with inlaid wood floors—along with elaborate plasterwork and gold-leaf decorations—create a sumptuous decor that was meant to show off the successes of a self-made man who was ennobled by the emperor and made a baron, a man whose family motto was "Honor, Reflection, Perseverance." His home, a private palace and showpiece during the baron's life, became a unique museum when it was preserved intact at his death.

ABOVE *Double columns with Ionic capitals frame the entrance to the luxuriously decorated dining room.*

LEFT AND FAR LEFT *Marble statues stand in mirrored niches in a small boudoir.*

LEFT *In the inlaid marble hall is a marble sculpture by Magni. This allegorical piece refers to the baron's contribution to the opening of the Suez Canal.*

BELOW *Marquetry of semiprecious stones depicts garlands of flowers.*

The selection of leather-bound books in the ground-floor library is a witness to Revoltella's many interests. The double bronze chandelier, the heavily carved, velvet-covered table and chairs, and the elaborate wood paneling contribute to the feeling of intimacy and reflection.

Temples of Learning

Since the end of the 16th century, Prague has been endowed with a number of prestigious libraries that speak to the erudition of its citizens. Today, two of these high repositories of knowledge astonish us with the immensity of their proportions and their grandiose decors. The Clementinum, a school founded by the Jesuits in 1556, was transformed into a university 100 years later. In 1727, a magnificently decorated room was built by Frantisek Maxmilian Kanka to house some of the university's most ancient volumes. The library, a Baroque masterpiece, is known for the beauty of its rococo painted ceilings and its collection of globes.

Included in the Strahov Library's collection of rare manuscripts is the Strahov Gospel, illuminated in the 9th and 10th centuries. The library's Philosophical Hall was constructed around a series of superb bookcases that came from the abbey at Louka. The delicate pilasters and borders, ornate balustrade, walnut shelves, and late-18th-century frescoed ceiling by F. A. Maulbertsch—depicting the "History of Humanity"—not only contribute to the room's awesome atmosphere but illustrate the high esteem in which books and manuscripts—considered the rare treasures of their time—were held.

LEOPOLDSKRON

Lake Views

The Baroque castle of Leopoldskron was built between 1736 and 1744 by Bernhard Stuart for Prince Archbishop Leopold Anton Freiherr von Firmian. Set on the shores of Lake Leopoldskron, facing the Untersberg Mountain from which the red and yellow marbles of Salzburg are quarried, the castle presents a facade that is stately and also rather playful.

A ceremonial marble staircase rises to the second floor where the grand reception rooms have a wit and impertinence about them. Figures from the commedia dell'arte are skillfully portrayed in gilded cartouches, candlelight is reflected in the mirrors, and the feeling is one of celebration.

From 1918 to 1938, Leopoldskron was the property of Max Reinhardt, the well-known theater director who founded the Salzburg Music Festival. Here he welcomed an international coterie of writers, artists, and musicians.

ABOVE *The Baroque facade of Leopoldskron was designed to have an imposing presence from across the lake.*

LEFT *The wrought-iron gates of Leopoldskron set between a pair of winged horses open onto the frozen lake and the snowcapped Untersberg Mountain.*

ABOVE AND ABOVE RIGHT *The walls in what was the archbishop's private dining room are decorated with fanciful rococo stucco reliefs, some of which frame 18th-century Italian paintings.*

RIGHT *On the landing, painted panels are inset into the window frames. The floor is of red and white marble squares.*

ABOVE *Painted marble busts stand on pedestals on the first-floor landing.*

RIGHT *A perspective of intersecting vaults and buttresses with gold-painted plasterwork can be seen above the majestic staircase.*

The Venetian Room boasts an inlaid parquet floor, silver-mirrored walls, and a large Venetian crystal chandelier. Venetian paintings of characters from the commedia dell'arte are set in elaborate gilded cartouches.

61

Antique engravings are set into the paneling of a small antechamber between the landing and the Venetian Room.

ABOVE AND RIGHT *The Baroque-style library—with its columned and pedimented bookcases, swirling gallery, and elaborate plasterwork—was designed and built for Max Reinhardt in 1927.*

OPPOSITE *The decor of the main salon was executed in the Chinese taste of the 18th century, with a chinoiserie chandelier and hand-painted wallpaper panels.*

Graceful Greenhouse

The *Palmenhaus*, or Palm House, in the garden at Schönbrunn—once the summer residence of the Austrian emperor, near Vienna—is one of the largest and most spectacular greenhouses in the world. Designed by Franz von Segenschmid in 1879, the graceful steel structure, *far left and above,* is an example of the marriage between form and function that characterizes the late 19th century. The surrounding gardens, *left,* combine a sense of classical French geometry with a freer, more romantic feeling in garden design.

NEUWARTENBURG

Imperial Hunting Lodge

Situated in the countryside outside Salzburg, Neuwartenburg is an 18th-century castle built by Johann Guyard, Count of St. Julien, the falconmaster at the court of Emperor Charles VI.

The elegant domed building was completed in 1732 and designed by Johann Erhard Martinelli, an Italian architect, in the Baroque style, which was popular in the aristocratic circles of the day. With its dependencies and outbuildings, the castle rises like a brilliant sun in the often overcast and gray landscape. The wide courtyard and long drive assured ceremonial arrivals and returns from the hunt.

The large reception rooms with their Baroque stoves look the same as they did when royalty came to visit, accompanied by their entourages. Although these were bucolic excursions, the formalism of the court was not forgotten. Originally, Neuwartenburg was used only occasionally to entertain hunting parties. Now, it is the year-round home of Elisabeth Gräfin Strachwitz, who inherited the castle and its lands in 1977.

With its striking yet simple proportions, the hunting castle and its dependencies are set around a welcoming central courtyard.

RIGHT *The approach to the 18th-century castle begins with a long allée of linden trees. The gate is capped with urns and dancing putti that emphasize the idea of relaxation and frolic at the castle.*

FAR RIGHT *Italian stucco detailing was the inspiration for the ornamentation on the courtyard wall.*

In the library, a collection of 18th-century English engravings has been set in gilded frames on the wood-paneled walls that have been installed in a pattern resembling parquet.

RIGHT *The table in the dining room has been covered with an antique Persian carpet. The monumental ceramic and gold-decorated stove dates from the early 18th century.*

FAR RIGHT *The grand entrance foyer was the place where the booty from the hunt was presented. The elaborate gilded coat of arms above the fireplace denotes the imperial status of the lodge.*

BELOW RIGHT AND BELOW FAR RIGHT *An unusual triangular table and cane chairs furnish the game room.*

A spectacular 18th-century marquetry armoire stands in the antechamber.

Electrical wires are strung like garlands in the antechamber, so as not to damage the walls with their original paint.

The walls of the sitting room
that was once reserved for
ladies are paneled in rosewood.
The bouquets of flowers set in
gilded frames are made of silk
appliqués and emphasize the
room's feminine ambience.

The Rural Life

In contrast with the changes and upheavals that defined life in the urban centers, life in the rural areas of Mittel Europa had an immutable quality. A wooden church, was a symbol of constancy and stability. There was not only a permanence of style but a strong repetition of domestic mores. From the 17th to the 20th centuries, the same rhythms endured.

Interiors of farmhouses, from the modest one-room cottage to the more elaborate two-story dwelling, have many elements in common.

The main living space was always focused around the stove, a masonry affair often covered in glazed ceramic tile. Baking was done in the hottest part, clothes were hung around it to dry, a bench next to it provided a place to keep warm while mending socks or peeling potatoes. Two stoves in one house often indicated the presence of multiple generations under one roof. In the humblest houses, there was only one room in which to live, to cook, to sleep, to work. If the house had a second floor, the room located directly above the stove was the warmest, and thus its occupants were deemed the most important in the household—hence the main or master bedroom.

Today, we look at these country abodes and their furnishings with an eye toward appreciating their intrinsic simplicity: the textures and colors of planks and beams worn by time, the bold patterns on a painted chest that held a bride's trousseau, the primitive shape of a glazed jug.

A wooden church in Slovakia.

Torysky is a village in the mountains of East Slovakia, near Levoca. More than many others in the countryside, this village has been able to preserve its time-honored rituals and customs.

But what makes this village even more unusual is the way its older inhabitants have continued to live as their parents and grandparents did—dressed in the traditional costumes of the region, in modest houses that line the main dirt road. They still farm and celebrate their holidays, just as they always have in the past.

LEFT *Head scarves, aprons, and smocked blouses of colorful printed and patterned cotton are part of the traditional everyday dress of the village women.*

ABOVE *Faded paper edges the trim above the door that separates the kitchen from the dining room.*

ABOVE RIGHT *Methylene-dyed whitewash gives the stove its blue cast. Cooking and heating is still done with wood.*

LEVOCA

Old Country Customs

ABOVE *A village woman sits in her kitchen in a traditional pose near the stove that provides heat for the house and on which her pots simmer.*

RIGHT *On the wall, between two religious images, is a souvenir of the husband of one of the women, Peter Barbustak's military service from 1934 to 1936.*

ABOVE *In the poorer houses, the kitchen, bedroom, and dining room are all the same room.*

ABOVE *In her bedroom, an old woman sits by the window. The bench allows her to spend hours looking out, which is her only occupation. The floors are covered with rugs woven in customary plaid patterns.*

ABOVE *Down-filled pillows and duvets, covered in red and blue mattress ticking, are stored on an unused bed in the one-room house. A sewing machine is near the window.*

RIGHT *The vintage Bakelite radio—still in working order—is the only modern touch in the house. It sits on a small shelf edged with a piece of cross-stitch embroidery made years ago by the woman of the house.*

Coffee mugs, hand-painted plates, and framed religious images are all intermingled in the decor. Statuettes of angels and saints are arranged on the window frame.

From the Forest

A large part of the landscape of Mittel Europa is covered with forest. Wood—mainly oak and beech—was both plentiful and cheap and did not need to be transported long distances. In the countryside of Slovakia and Bohemia, the houses seem to be as one with the landscape. Construction methods, whether post-and-beam or timber-frame, along with thatch roofs and woven wood, have been repeated for centuries. Wood has been a rich source for creativity. Roofs and gates, balconies and doors, window frames and walls, have been interpreted by craftsmen, who, while working in different countries, retained a kinship as to the perpetuity of their craft.

Today, these wood-crafted houses and farm buildings remain as testimony to a diminishing folk art tradition.

The early-19th-century farmhouse was originally built on a sloping mountain site.

Two-Family Farmhouse

The Peter House was originally constructed in 1818 in Weiler Waidach, near Nussdorf on the slopes of the Haunsberg Mountains. It has been moved to the Salzburger Freilichtmuseum, outside Salzburg. The two-family farmhouse can be entered either from the back, directly into the main living floor, or up a flight of steps that was built to accommodate the house's original sloping site.

There are two kitchens with ceramic-tiled, wood-burning masonry stoves. One was for the older generation's use when the children took over the running of the farm. The open ovens were used up to World War II. A third stove in the living room was used in the winter months for cooking. Upstairs were the unheated bedrooms, with the south side of the house occupied by the retired farmer and the northern rooms for his heirs, probably because the southern exposure afforded more warmth.

LEFT AND BELOW *The two kitchens in the house accommodated the older and younger generations that lived there.*

When the bedrooms were not occupied, the bedclothes (including the thick duvets) were hung on a rope stretched across the room, for airing and to avoid the effects of humidity. Several members of the same family shared the bedrooms.

The master bedroom is glimpsed through a door that is framed with a cutout wood design. The sparse room is furnished only with a painted bed, chest, and rag rugs.

The large armoires have been painted with traditional geometric and floral patterns. Like the chests, they held the family's most precious belongings, and often the daughters' trousseaux. Women often painted the pieces, sometimes portraying the village in which they lived.

Country Inn

In the fertile region bounded by Prague, the Ore Mountains, and the mountains of central Bohemia is the village of Trebiz. The complex of farm buildings that once belonged to the Cifka family stands on the village green near the pond.

Originally constructed in the 16th century, it was rebuilt many times until the wealthy family of farmers turned it into a country inn at the turn of this century. Today it is one of a few of the most admirable houses of Trebiz that have been opened to the public. The light streaming into the dining room where the table is covered with a heavy white linen cloth and the stately four-poster bed that anchors the spacious bedroom give the illusion that the rooms are simply waiting for the next occupants to arrive.

ABOVE LEFT *The farmhouse, with its typical yellow and white facade, was built around a courtyard with a high arched entrance. There was a door used by visitors arriving on foot; a gate was to receive the carriages and horses.*

LEFT *The two-story building with its exterior staircase dates from the 19th century.*

ABOVE *The front door opens into the courtyard. The wood staircase leads to the bedrooms. The dining room is two steps up from the hall.*

LEFT *The parquet floor, the urbane chairs and table, and the family portraits on the wall attest to the new wealth of the farm family.*

The spacious and austere bedroom, which also boasts a parquet floor and double doors, is furnished with a four-poster bed and a cast-iron stove.

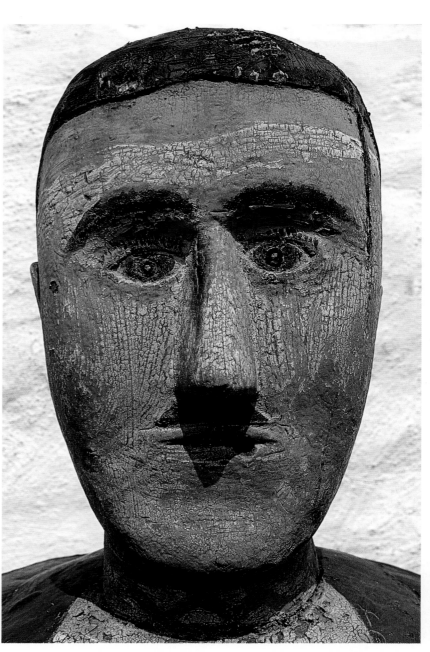

Rural Settlement

EAST SLOVAKIA

The wood-beam cottages with their straw-and-earth mortar dyed blue with methylene were built at the turn of the century in Velky Lipnik. Their traditional furnishings were used until recently, when they were moved to the village of Stara Lubovna to be part of a *skansen*, or open-air museum, near Poprad, a large town in East Slovakia. As in many other rural houses, the table was a focus of the room, with the stove the second place around which the family liked to gather. These wood-beam houses join other rural buildings that have been moved from villages in the area to illustrate Slovakia's mix of cultures, including Slovak, German, and Greek Orthodox influences.

Traveling workmen, tinkers, and toy sellers, along with itinerant peddlers, brought such wares as Bohemian paintings on glass to Slovakia and Hungary. The folk art traditions that originated in the different areas then found themselves mingled in a house that would be passed down from generation to generation.

OPPOSITE *The two heads belong to life-size figures of a man and a woman, which were carved by local people to be used for festivals.*

ABOVE *On the interior of one of the houses, the wood beams have been left exposed, just as they are on the exterior. Religious engravings line the wall of the dining room,* above left. *The painted chest,* left, *celebrated the marriage of Katarina to Palein in 1913. A plain glass-fronted buffet holds the everyday pottery.*

Paper edging trims one of the beams in the dining room where cups are hung. Three Greek Orthodox icons are displayed on the beam below. A kerosene lamp provides light.

The bedroom and kitchen are one, so as to
take advantage of the heat of the stove in
the harsh mountainous region.

In another house, the beds are covered with cotton spreads embroidered with traditional motifs or with red-and-white-striped ticking. A painted chest was the usual piece of furniture found at the foot of the bed. Narrow rag rugs are usually the only coverings on the floor. Finishing the walls was considered a luxury.

Country Churches

In all the different countries of Mittel Europa, the country church was often made of wood—spruce for the main structure, oak and beech for the belfries.

Shingle was used for the roofs, and the ornamentation was stylistically influenced by both Western and Eastern Byzantine styles. While the older churches, some of which date from the 15th century, reflect elements of Gothic style, many of the later churches have ground plans in the form of the Greek cross.

In the countryside of Bohemia in particular, even the smallest village church reflected the Baroque architecture of the day as it was seen in the grand edifices that flourished in the large cities.

Blacksmith's Modernized House

FLACHGAU

In the late 19th century, what was originally a single-family farmhouse from the Flachgau region near Salzburg was converted into a home and workshop for a blacksmith. Some of the old wood walls were replaced with brick; the living room became a forge.

While most of the original wood structure of the second floor was preserved, the wood balcony was replaced with a wrought-iron railing. The roof over the main living quarters was covered in cement shingles, a material that appeared in the area around 1900.

The electrical installation is also modern. The ceramic and Bakelite switches and outlets, with their twisted cotton-covered wires strung along walls, now give an old-fashioned decorative touch though the arrangement is purely functional.

LEFT *The farmhouse—with its new electrical installation, wallpapered or roller-stenciled walls, and white lacquered furniture—has a rather urban feeling.*

RIGHT *The freestanding wood-burning stove is a modern version of the built-in masonry unit. A tin chimney replaces the stone conduit.*

ABOVE *The ceramic light switch was applied to a wall on which a pattern was painted with a roller—a turn-of-the-century decorative innovation.*

RIGHT *The master bedroom is furnished with beds, an armoire, a chest and storage cabinet, and a bedside table that have been lacquered white. The successive coats of paint give the surface of the furniture a soft, rounded look. The use of high beds in the low-ceilinged room was to take advantage of the heat from the stove in the room below.*

Farm Families

OPPOSITE *The Knotzingerhaus, built in 1798, was originally the main house on an estate in the Flachgau region.*

LEFT AND BELOW *The Bichlaiden house dates from 1666 and was constructed entirely of wood. Long galleries edged with fretwork stretch across the facade.*

The Salzburger Freilichtmuseum, situated at the foot of the Untersberg Mountain, a few miles outside Salzburg, groups together a series of farmhouses and farm buildings that come from the five most important provinces of the nine that make up the Salzburg region. The buildings and their grounds offer a glimpse into the life and evolution of rural life over three centuries.

The houses came from the countryside between the Alpenvorland and the Central Alps and reflect the German Bavarian, Celtic Roman, and Slavic heritages of the region.

The three houses shown span from the second half of the 17th century to the late 1830s. Although all rustic in style, they parallel the economic differences of the families that lived in them. The plank wood wall became stucco; the rough-hewn wood bed was transformed into a floral-patterned work of folk art; and the plain storage trunk was replaced with a sophisticated painted chest.

LEFT AND RIGHT *One of the bedrooms on the second floor of the Knotzingerhaus has been furnished with a bed and a wedding chest painted with floral motifs typical of the Alpine region. The eye on the headboard is meant to guard against bad luck.*

FAR RIGHT AND BELOW RIGHT *In a 17th-century Bichlaiden house, the rough wood walls are typical of a modest home. The minimally furnished master bedroom has two single beds, placed in a symmetrical and traditional arrangement.*

The ground floor of the Hiertlhaus, built in 1836, includes a dining room furnished with a banquette that lines two walls. A corner shelf, on which hangs a piece of embroidery, holds the traditional religious images and artifacts. Linens are hung up to dry in front of the stove, which is covered in green ceramic tiles. Plates, some of which come from Gmunden, are stored in the wall-hung dish-holder.

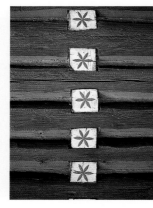

Colorful Pattern

I n most of Slovakia, particularly in the mountainous areas, there has been a long tradition of building in wood.

In the northeast, near the Polish border and especially around the village of Zdiar in the High Tatras, many villages developed an individualistic approach to the decoration of their log houses.

The motifs were often inspired by traditional embroidery patterns. Doors, window frames, shutters, and the exposed surfaces where the structural wood beams joined at the corners were the prime surfaces targeted for the colorful and imaginative designs.

In the Adobe Manner

BARDEJOV

Located in northeast Slovakia, the town of Bardejov still retains the medieval feeling it developed when it was settled by Germans in the 14th century and flourished as a trading and crafts center between Hungary, Poland, and Russia.

Nearby is the Bardejovske Kupele, a spa surrounded by forests, which is also the site of an open-air museum with old buildings similar to adobes, structures made from sun-dried bricks of clay and straw, that have been moved there from villages in the outlying regions.

The thatched roof of the adobe-style house is characteristic of the buildings that come from the villages on the southeastern slope of the Vihorlat mountain.

*A ladder is used to reach the hayloft,
where the corn for the winter was stored.*

*A hanging kerosene lamp lights the dim
and simply furnished dining room.*

ABOVE AND ABOVE RIGHT *The bedroom, kitchen, and living room are all in the same space. The table is set between the two beds. Under one of the beds is a couchette, or trundle bed, that was pulled out for children to sleep in.*

ABOVE *The masonry wood stove in one of the houses has been stenciled with geometric patterns. The pine boughs would have been used as kindling.*

RIGHT *The arrangement of furniture in the main living space, which also functioned as a bedroom, was the same in many small towns and villages.*

Bohemian Folk Art

The village of Kourim, located near Prague, is situated in a large apple orchard in the hilly landscape that is characteristic of central Bohemia.

The large wood houses, with their two stories, their windows framed with fanciful designs, and their richly decorated cupboards and four-poster beds, reflect the more comfortable way of life that was due to the area's fertile and well-developed agriculture.

OPPOSITE FAR LEFT *The white-painted ornamented window frames and whitewashed mortar between the beams give the exterior a strong graphic look.*

ABOVE *A richly painted cupboard stands on the stone floor in the entrance hall of the wood house.*

OPPOSITE AND ABOVE *The intricate motifs that are part of a long-standing tradition are either repetitive patterns or more free floral designs that are based on the richness of the natural landscape.*

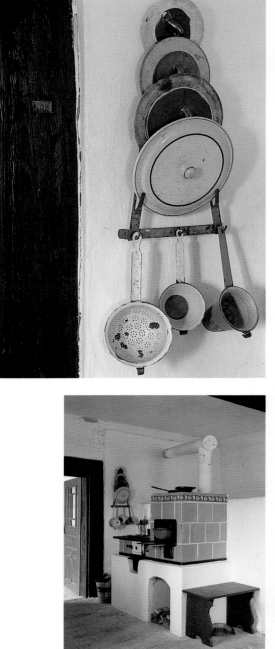

TOP *Pot covers and enamel utensils are stored on a metal rack near the stove.*

ABOVE *The blue and white ceramic-tile stove is the focus of the kitchen.*

ABOVE *The two-piece painted cupboard is meant to hold the everyday plates.*

ABOVE *In the dining room, the crucifix is placed atop the corner cupboard. The paintings under glass are all religious images hung, as is traditional, on the two walls near the table.*

TOP *Wooden implements are kept in a wire holder crafted by an itinerant artisan in Slovakia about 100 years ago.*

ABOVE *The four-poster bed has a charmingly painted headboard, footboard, and canopy. The white cotton bedcover has been finished with openwork embroidery.*

Baroque-Style Farmhouses

Once only rustic farmhouses dotted the Bohemian countryside. But over the centuries the proximity of the cosmopolitan city of Prague as well as the evolution of the status of the farmers led to the development of a new style of vernacular architecture.

Under the strong influence of what was the reigning Baroque style in the large cities of Mittel Europa in the early 18th century, people felt the need to start to embellish their houses. Generations of talented local craftsmen decorated the large farmhouses with sunshine-topped portals and applied a diversity of three-dimensional decorative motifs to the already gracefully ornate facades.

The nearly exclusively yellow-and-white combinations that contrasted the building's facade with its ornamentation, recalling the Italian Baroque palette, give the surrounding landscape a joyous, lighthearted look that is still appreciated today.

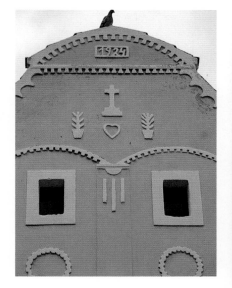

A Collector's Treasures

Hungary's rich traditions of decorative folk art—its painted cupboards, utilitarian pottery, and colorful weavings—have until the last two decades been appreciated only by specialized collectors. One of the most refined collections of Hungarian folk art belongs to a doctor who lives in the countryside near Budapest. His modest home is a miniature museum of the diverse crafts that developed in the different regions of the country.

All of the objects displayed there are of the highest quality and were collected at a time when it was still possible to find objects in the villages where they were made and used for generations. Crowded on shelves or displayed in profusion on the walls, the once-utilitarian objects have taken on a decorative quality that is enhanced by the varieties of patterns and design expressions: on a ceramic tile, round plate, or jaunty pot.

ABOVE LEFT *Traditional pitchers in the shape of mustachioed men are stored in a cupboard painted with floral motifs.*

LEFT *Storage jars, pitchers, and pots, some of which were once used for cooking and were crafted in Transylvania, are lined up atop a cupboard dated 1847.*

RIGHT *Thick glazed terra-cotta tiles, almost all the typically green ones that were used for building stoves, are now grouped one by one on the wall.*

The landing at the top of the stair is where the plates—most of which were made in Transylvania—are on display. Originally, they would have been used every day and stored in a wall rack or hung with string on the wall.

*The bedroom, with its painted cupboard
and chest, and woven wall hangings, is in
the style of a popular house. Pieces of
pottery line the high shelves.*

The Bourgeois Manner

L ong before the word *Biedermeier* became associated with a 19th-century furniture style, it was synonymous with an attitude that considered comfort and respectability the prime virtues of society. *Bieder* means "honest" and maybe a little dull; *Meier* was a very common surname. To be an "honest bourgeois" was to be on a straight path.

The Biedermeier style that was born in Vienna in the first decades of the 19th century became an art of living rather than an inventive decorative revolution. Pioneering furniture makers, such as Danhauser in Vienna, not only offered dozens of different chair designs, illustrated in cataloglike drawings, but could also produce the myriad pieces in quantity.

With the development of trade and industry in the second half of the 19th century, a new bourgeoisie was establishing itself and exerting its influence in cultural and political circles. Their homes and apartments grew in proportion to their new wealth and power in society. A whole new cosmopolitan lifestyle emerged. Trieste grew to prominence as a trading port open to international commerce. Leisure and sporting activities, taking the waters at grandiose thermal establishments, and vacationing in luxurious hotels became a way of life.

Although their appeal has diminished over the years, today many grand hotels and spas are being appreciated anew, both for their architecture and the Old World amenities they offer to a generation that is now ready to rediscover their charms.

An old-fashioned hat shop in Prague.

Biedermeier Beauty

ABOVE *The turquoise-blue ceramic stove in the main entrance hall was made in Vienna about 1820.*

RIGHT *The summer house, with Gothic Revival arches and a columned veranda, was conceived as a variation on a traditional garden pavilion.*

RIGHT *Because of its Arabic decorations, one of the anterooms is known as "the mosque." The alabaster statue is from the mid-19th century.*

I n what was once the countryside outside Vienna, the
house that is known today as
the Geymüllerschlössel was
built at the beginning of the
19th century as a summer
home for Johann Jakob Gey-
müller, a Viennese banker. The
architect, whose name is unknown, was inspired by the garden follies of the time, and he
incorporated Gothic and Arabic
elements into the design of the
eccentric building.

After a century of splendor,
the house fell into decay and
neglect. But in 1945 Franz
Sobek bought the property and
restored the house and its gardens. He also filled the rooms
with his collections of Viennese clocks and enviable Empire and Biedermeier pieces.
Sobek donated the house to the
Republic of Austria in 1965.

Recently, under the direction
of Christian Witt-Dörring, cu-
rator at the Austrian Museum
of Applied Arts in Vienna, the
rooms were redecorated and the
furniture reupholstered in as
authentic a way as possible so
as to re-create the atmosphere
of an Empire Biedermeier house.

ABOVE AND LEFT *One of the salons, with its 1820 Viennese ceramic stove, has been decorated with a scenic Zuber wallpaper that is a reproduction of an original 1806 design called Hindustan. The suite of furniture—of ebonized wood with bronzed paste decorations—was made in Vienna by the Danhauser Mobelfabrik in around 1815. The upholstery was redone after what was believed to be the original covering.*

LEFT *In the middle of the dining room is a mahogany table made in Vienna in about 1825. Surrounding it is a set of 1830s mahogany chairs with maple veining. The two chairs against the wall are of maple with pen decorations and date from about 1815. The clocks are part of Sobek's collection of 160 Viennese timepieces that date from the 1770s to the 1870s.*

RIGHT *The solid and veneered mahogany chair, upholstered in silk, was made in Vienna about 1815.*

ABOVE *The walnut lady's desk in the cupola room was made in Vienna about 1825, as were the chairs. The two containers on either side of the desk are meant for plants. The étagère in the background is called a* servante, *an archaic word for vitrine.*

LEFT *The chandelier in the cupola room is an 1820 Vienna design. It used to hang in the Albertina, once the winter town palace of the Archduke Charles, brother of Emperor Francis I. The 1840 settee has been reupholstered in an English chintz. The table is an 1815 Danhauser design, with a top of veneered mahogany; the base is of wood painted green to look like patinated bronze, with applied gilded paste decorations. The chairs, made in Vienna around 1825, have been upholstered in a style typical of the later 19th century.*

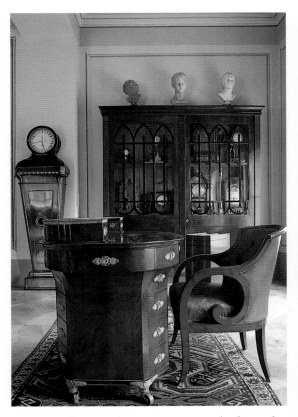

ABOVE *The Danhauser writing desk in the yellow and purple drawing room dates from about 1820. It was made for the Weilburg Palace, the summer residence of the Archduke Charles, outside Vienna. The mahogany and ormolu chair is Viennese and dates from about 1825.*

RIGHT *The stained pearwood and ormolu seating, upholstered in emerald silk, in the anteroom on the second floor was made around 1805 for the Empress Maria Ludovica, second wife of the Emperor Franz. The table is French and dates from about 1820. The pictures of flowers on the wall are of porcelain. The tall candelabra on either side of the settee are from Vienna and date from about 1820.*

145

ABOVE *The superb cylindrical writing desk in the drawing room is dated and signed "Haerle 1813."*

LEFT *The mahogany furniture in the yellow and purple drawing room was made by Danhauser in about 1825. Silk was specially woven in Florence for the upholstery, which is a reproduction of the original design. The carpet is a French Aubusson from the mid-19th century. The subject of the late 1830s portrait is unknown.*

RIGHT *The 1800 lady's worktable is of burlwood with polished steel and marcasite detailing. All the original implements for sewing and painting are still in it.*

RIGHT AND BELOW RIGHT *In the dining room, the curved moldings have been painted white to contrast with the yellow and gray walls. Candles, placed either in the footed wrought-iron candle stand or in the 18th-century gilded candelabra that stands on a small table, are often used for atmosphere in the evening.*

BELOW *Vintage photographs, an unusual globe, and a book of nautical flags are displayed in the study.*

Many of the families that became wealthy in Trieste at the beginning of the 19th century owed their fortunes to the rapid development of the international trade and maritime businesses that flourished at that time. The Rossetti family—whose members included the founders of Lloyd Triestino, the shipping company—has kept alive its links to its origins in the navigation industry. The grand apartment still belongs to the family. Once considered conventional with its old-fashioned layout and rather stiff reception rooms, it has survived to become an unusual example of its kind.

Few such apartments—with a grand entrance hall and ante-chambers *en suite*—still remain whole. And even when they do, the way of life that unfolded in the rooms has been simplified and is just a memory of what it once was.

BELOW LEFT *The windows in the living room include stained-glass panels instead of draperies to provide privacy. Outside, Italian-style wood shutters protect the interior from the bright sun.*

RIGHT *The austere dove-gray living room is furnished with early-18th-century pieces. A chinoiserie painting hangs on the wall.*

Shipping Heritage

In the fall, rugs that have been rolled up during the summer months are put back in place. The Louis XIV armchairs in the dining room have been covered with a tapestry fabric in a flame pattern. The ornate fireplace is a hybrid between a classic Italian mantelpiece and a traditional ceramic stove.

Taking the Waters

Since Roman times, the spa has been the place for people to go for medicinal and relaxation purposes. Certain waters were thought to heal different sicknesses, from heart and circulation ailments to rheumatism and arthritis. The Turkish *hamam* became the epitome of luxurious bathing. Today, in Budapest, the 16th-century Kiraly Bath is the last relic from the city's Turkish domination.

By the middle of the 19th century, with the evolution of the rich bourgeoisie, a large number of spas in Budapest—but also in the countryside of Hungary, Austria, Slovakia, and Bohemia—were touting the medicinal properties of their respective waters.

The needs of the new clientele taking the cure included a sophisticated social life, with entertainments and promenades in formal gardens, where orchestras in kiosks played every afternoon. This justified the creation of a special style of architecture. And the grand hotel, the lavish garden, and the exuberant thermal establishment reached its apotheosis.

In western Bohemia, Karlovy Vary (also known as Karlsbad) is set in a valley along the river Teplá and framed by forest-covered hills. In competition with Marianske Lazne (or Marienbad) Karlovy Vary, *these pages*, was *the* place for the upper classes to take the waters.

Budapest's medicinal hot springs, with temperatures from 22°C (72°F) to 76°C (168°F), which have been famous since antiquity, are known as the richest of all the world's large cities.

Even today, there are more than 30 bathhouses, including swimming pools, that are open to the public. The Gellert Baths, these pages, with its 13 sources of water, designed by Armin Hegedus, Artur Sebestyen, and Izidor Stark in 1918, is one of the most extraordinary spas in the world.

Built in the art nouveau style entirely of ceramic tile, with exquisite mosaic patterns that form a background for Turkish baths, swimming pools, and resting areas for both men and women, the Gellert Baths is a monumental expression of the richness and originality of this decorative style.

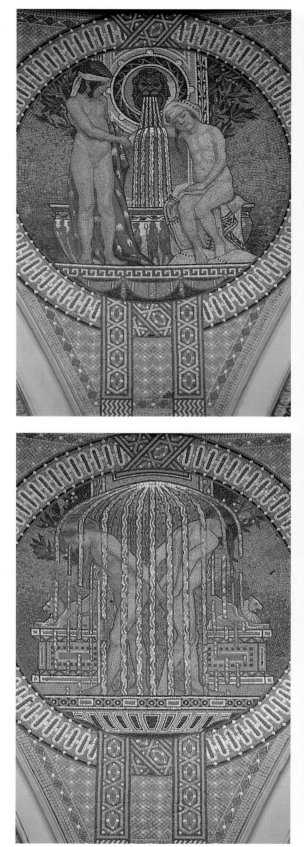

BELOW AND RIGHT *Tall doors open to reveal a series of reception and private rooms en enfilade.*

Cosmopolitan Setting

TRIESTE

Palazzo Morpurgo, in the center of Trieste, is one of the last remaining witnesses to life in a grand family home at the turn of the century.

The house once belonged to one of Trieste's wealthiest bourgeois families. Commissioned in 1857, it was one of the most grandiose residences of its time. Ensconced behind a gold-decorated facade are a series of suites where velvet draperies, crystal chandeliers, and Venetian mirrors created a backdrop for a cosmopolitan life. Unfortunately, the important collections of china, glass, paintings, and books could not be saved intact from the upheavals of the Second World War. At his death in 1947, Mario Morpurgo de Nilma—who was the last to inherit the entire building as well as its immense apartment—gave the property to the city of Trieste in order to preserve it.

Even though the rooms are now empty, the sense of what life was like in the opulent-but-lived-in rooms still remains. One can nearly hear the tinkle of wineglasses and the animated conversations that once filled the house. One can still imagine the kitchen, now sparkling clean and quiet, as a bustle of activity. With its scrubbed floors and off-white-painted furniture, it is as evocative of its time as the much grander salons.

RIGHT *The music room has been decorated in the style of Louis XIV as it was interpreted in the second half of the 19th century. The piano is a Bosendorfer.*

ABOVE *The heavily carved chairs upholstered in tooled leather in the dining room are typical of the 1880s. A large gilt mirror hangs above the white majolica mantelpiece.*

RIGHT *The small boudoir is known as the* Salotto Azzurro, *or "Blue Sitting Room." The mantelpiece is of white Carrara marble, the chandelier of Venetian glass. All the tufted seating is covered in pale blue silk to match the draperies. The engravings depicting elegant ladies further emphasize the feminine aura of the room.*

A huge gilt and crystal chandelier from Bohemia hangs in the center of the large music room, the most grandiose space in the apartment. Red-damask-covered gilt chairs are grouped around a series of tables. Two gilt and crystal candelabra are reflected in the mirror above the mantelpiece.

The Sala d'Angolo, or "Corner Sitting Room," is more austere. The oval table and chests are red, black, and gold boulle pieces. The gilt bronze candelabrum with its French porcelain decorations adds a note of color.

The Salottino Nero, *or "Small Black Sitting Room," is furnished with inlaid wood pieces. The 18th-century paintings by an anonymous artist are copies of portraits and self-portraits of famous Italian men. The originals are in the Uffizi gallery in Florence.*

LEFT *The library and study was Baron Morpurgo's favorite room. The walnut bookcase with glass doors is filled with books in different languages that reflect the family's numerous interests.*

BELOW LEFT *The large master bedroom is furnished with a pair of half-tester oak beds. A pair of ancestral portraits hang above the sofa.*

In the study, low chairs
upholstered in velvet and
fringed are pulled up to an
intricately carved Anglo-
Indian table.

A family portrait with an
ornate frame of gilded leaves is
in a corner of the long corridor
that runs about the perimeter
of the apartment.

ABOVE *The white-tiled bathroom with its pedestal sink and opaline accessories is identical to those found in many luxurious apartments of the time.*

ABOVE AND ABOVE RIGHT *A glass door separates the corridor from the old-fashioned blue and white kitchen.*

LEFT *The three stoves that stand side by side are an indication of the scale of activities that once took place here.*

ABOVE *Copper cake and jelly molds hang on hooks above a worktable.*

Records of a City

From 1832 to 1856, the records of the city of Vienna were under the direction of Franz Grillparzer, a popular playwright, poet, and philosopher. Kept in thick volumes, the archives of the Imperial Treasury were grouped sequentially and marked with the years to which they correspond. The records were filed in a maze of atmospherically dark rooms in an 18th-century mansion designed by Daniel Dietrich on Vienna's Johannesgasse.

Grillparzer's office, *above left,* was furnished in the Biedermeier style that was popular in the mid-19th century. As is typical of many Viennese sitting rooms, a high table has been placed in front of the sofa. Tall armoires hold books and papers, and a stool can be pulled up to a standing desk. At the rear, the long writing table is equipped with a pull-up shade for privacy. An open volume in the archive, *below left,* includes samples from all the textile weavers who worked in Vienna in the 17th century.

The archive, where the thick books can be studied at long tables, looks exactly as it did in Grillparzer's time. Records that go back to the 13th century, including documents on religion, trade, and legal matters, are stacked on floor-to-ceiling shelves. Wood ladders allow access to the high shelves. The archive is open for researchers whose areas of interest include the accounting books, trade registers, and statistics of the city of Vienna.

Mountain Resorts

With the industrial revolution that overtook Europe at the end of the 19th century came a new class of wealthy people who would soon develop their social habits and tastes. To fill their leisure time, satisfy their health concerns, and for a feeling of well-being, people began to experience nature and discover sporting activities.

Large new hotels and smaller cottages were built to meet the sophisticated demands of this new clientele. In the High Tatra Mountains of Slovakia, such resorts as Stary Smokovec, Zdiar, and Novy Smokovec were some of the first to become popular in Mittel Europa. Visitors came from Prague and Vienna, as well as the larger cities of Poland and Germany.

The turn-of-the-century houses in which the bourgeoisie spent their holidays have a style of their own, incorporating the wood architecture typical of Swiss chalets, with its applied edelweiss motifs, the Victorian gingerbread fretwork of the porches, and the brilliant range of colors that were inspired by the distinctive folk art of the region.

Country Villa

Set in the Cacciatore, a wooded area where Trieste's most notable inhabitants used to spend their summers, the late-19th-century Villa Revoltella is surrounded by a formal garden known both for the quantity and quality of its century-old trees. Built of wood and cast iron, the small house offered its occupants an easy-to-reach escape from the city.

Whereas in town the family resided in a mansion, when they went out to the country they chose to play in what they considered a cottage. Nowadays, the Gothic-style greenhouses are a little forlorn, but the Italian-influenced garden has retained its charm, mainly because of its more intimate scale.

TOP RIGHT *A cast-iron porch adorns the red-painted facade of the wood house.*

LEFT *Next to the formal garden, which has been laid out in the Italian manner, is a cast-iron Gothic Revival greenhouse.*

ABOVE *Cast-iron stairs and railings create a graphic pattern around the exterior.*

The Modern Vision

W hen in 1893 Otto Wagner won the competition for the plan for the new Vienna, he opened the door to the modern era. Wagner was also a pioneer of the Jugendstil—the Austrian equivalent of art nouveau, which championed the total integration of all the disciplines to create a unified whole.

The Vienna Secession, formed in 1897 as a reaction to the staid, monumental architecture of the time, included Joseph Maria Olbrich, the architect who designed the building known as the Secession, that design movement's most important symbol. With its glorious dome of interlaced gilded laurel leaves, it was the antithesis of the historicist architecture then celebrated in Vienna.

In 1903, Josef Hoffmann founded the Wiener Werkstätte, a crafts cooperative that was to continue some of the ideals of the Secession until 1932. He found himself in opposition to Adolf Loos, rationalist par excellence and enemy of ornament.

Between 1910 and 1920, Pavel Janák would translate his ideas into dramatic three-dimensional cubist facades. Alphonse Maria Mucha designed the first Czechbanknotes, and Franz Kafka wrote his *Metamorphosis*. Painters like Oskar Kokoschka and Egon Schiele, composers like Gustav Mahler and Arnold Schoenberg, writers like Stefan Zweig and Arthur Schnitzler, poets like Hugo von Hofmannsthal, as well as psychoanalyst Sigmund Freud and philosopher Ludwig Wittgenstein, were among the personalities who defined the culture of the period in Central Europe.

A facade by Otto Wagner in Vienna.

An Artist's Private Domain

Alphonse Maria Mucha—world-famous for his art nouveau commercial theater posters and advertising campaigns for champagne, cookies, and bicycles—was born in 1860 in Moravia. Although the artist spent most of his life in Paris, he never forgot his roots in the Czech culture.

Returning to Prague in 1910, Mucha created his monumental 20-painting oeuvre known as *The Saga of the Slavs.* He lived in an 18th-century house on a picturesque square near the Royal Palace and died there in 1929. Inhabited by members of his son's family, the house is still intact. A curious relic, filled with Mucha's personal collections of posters, paintings, and memorabilia, it is one of the few private homes in Prague to have kept its turn-of-the-century personality.

Poised between the formal and the bohemian, the layered interior offers a rich array of the artist's work in different media and an arcane assemblage of bits and pieces.

ABOVE *The 18th-century house faces a small square.*

LEFT *In the hall, a grouping of Mucha watercolors hangs above an 18th-century chest.*

BELOW *An eccentric collection of objects—including stuffed birds, a crucifix, and a skull— is arranged near a fireplace.*

OPPOSITE TOP *Two of Mucha's famous posters, commissioned by the actress Sarah Bernhardt for the Théâtre de la Renaissance in Paris, hang on either side of an ornate wrought-iron gate in the entrance. The poster for Victorien Sardou's* Gismonda, *on the left of the doorway, launched his career with Bernhardt. She had commissioned it for the 100th performance of the play. It quickly became a collector's piece.*

OPPOSITE BOTTOM *The style of the heavily carved neo-Renaissance furniture in the ground-floor dining room contrasts with the fluidity of Mucha's lyrical art nouveau posters.*

LEFT *In the hall, a grouping of Mucha watercolors hangs above an 18th-century chest.*

The comfortable living room on the second floor is cluttered with an assortment of 18th-century furniture, leather-bound books, and art nouveau silver and pottery. A harmonium anchors the corner where tea is taken. An elaborate gilded cheval mirror is in front of the window.

The photograph nestled in one of the bookcases in the living room is of Mucha with the painter Paul Gauguin, Annah La Javanaise, a well-known model, and Ludek Marold, a Czech painter.

Many of Mucha's paintings, prints, and drawings hang on the living room walls, which are covered in a rococo chinoiserie wallpaper. The large portrait to the right of the fireplace is of Mucha's wife, Maruska.

ABOVE *The extraordinary rose-shaped art nouveau lamp in the bedroom once belonged to Sarah Bernhardt.*

RIGHT *The painting that hangs above the door in the living room is of Mucha's daughter Jaroslaza.*

Artful Figures

Especially in Prague, sculpture is closely integrated with architecture, giving buildings a dynamic look that animates the facades that line the streets, from the most modest houses to the city's sumptuous palaces. At the turn of the century, modernist interpretations of these classical figures brought the marriage of art and architecture into the 20th century.

In Vienna, the Jugendstil further celebrated the individualistic and romantic point of view. Lyrical forms, floral designs, and exuberant decorations were added to the facade ornamentations that often depicted female figures in graceful poses, in mosaic and stone.

The Russian constructivist style that inserted itself in the architecture of Prague at the beginning of the 1920s and that paralleled the functionalist movement in Vienna between the two world wars influenced design in all of Central Europe, including such cities as Trieste. The figures that looked as if they were holding up balconies or framing pediments took on a more geometric and monumental air. Poetry gave way to austerity, lyricism to heroics.

Personal Patronage

I n 1906, Karl Wittgenstein, a brilliant careerist in the iron and steel industry, asked Josef Hoffmann, the Viennese architect whose reputation as one of the founders of the Wiener Werkstätte was already established (the building of the Palais Stoclet had begun in Brussels the year before), to redesign one of his family's modest hunting lodges in Hochreith in the forests of lower Austria.

One of the wealthiest industrialists in Austria and the father of eight children—the youngest of whom was Ludwig, who was to become the famous philosopher—Wittgenstein had retired from business in 1898 to devote himself to being a patron of the arts and became the most important supporter of the Viennese Secession.

The renovation of the country house was another way for Wittgenstein to champion the ideas of modernism, albeit on a small scale. Although Hoffmann's habit was often to create a *Gesamtkunstwerk,* or complete work of art, in keeping with the rustic feeling of the area the architect did not change the exterior of the house at all. But inside he created a completely innovative and unified modern decor. In its urbanity, the masterful and sophisticated interior contrasts with the rustic feeling of the lodge and its mountain setting.

ABOVE FAR LEFT *The red wood and stucco house is like many of the region—but only from the outside.*

ABOVE LEFT *Josef Hoffmann designed the wicker chairs and table specifically for the hunting lodge.*

LEFT *The view of the hills and valley stretches for miles.*

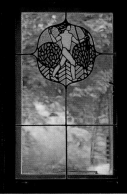

LEFT *The wood door of one of the lodge's outbuildings has been left rough-hewn.*

FAR LEFT AND ABOVE *The leaded stained-glass windows are by Koloman Moser, one of the leaders of the Wiener Werkstätte movement.*

LEFT *Hoffmann was the mastermind behind every detail of the interior, including the bronze medallion set into the paneling of the dining room, the lyrical painted door, ceramic stove, and the majolica panel that has been inset into the tiled wall in the alcove behind the stove, as well as the figure set into the stove itself.*

RIGHT *In the small foyer, a Hoffmann Wiener Werkstätte umbrella stand holds walking sticks and tennis rackets.*

The walls of the small combination dining and living room have been covered with a grid of marquetry panels outlined in brass. Hoffmann designed all the furniture that was originally in the room. But over the years some pieces were replaced, as is the case of the upholstered chairs.

ÖSTERR. POSTSPARKASSE·

198

Postal Savings Bank

Otto Wagner entered a competition in 1903 for the design of Vienna's Postsparkasse, or Postal Savings Bank, and won the commission over the 36 other entrants. Completed in 1912 and considered one of the masterpieces of 20th-century architecture, the huge building has a facade of thin marble slabs that have been bolted together, *left*.

Wagner also designed the interior and all of the details and furnishings, including the sculptural aluminum heating fixtures in the main hall, the stairwells and stair railings, and the tables and chairs in the waiting areas, *right*.

The boardroom is paneled in walnut that has been stained black. The chairs, a famous Wagner design that dates from 1906, were manufactured by the Gebrüder Thonet company.

Wagner's attention to detail is apparent in the elegant manner in which he treated the vents under the windows in the boardroom, as well as in his design for the built-in barometer.

The portrait of Emperor Franz Joseph I by Wilhelm List, one of the founders of the Secession movement, looms large over the long walnut and gray felt–covered table in the boardroom.

Café Society

At the turn of the century, in the centers of Eastern Europe—Vienna, Budapest, and Prague—and also in Trieste, the café quickly became an institution. It was the place to meet socially, to write, to read the newspapers that arrived from all over the world, and, most important, to exchange ideas. People stayed for hours, doing all these things, and sipping one of the many varieties of coffee offered: *Brauner*, with a little milk; *Kleine Schwarzer*, strong black; or *Mélange*, half-milk, half-coffee.

Many of these cafés were very well known. In Vienna, Sigmund Freud liked to frequent the Café Landtmann, and Leon Trotsky was often seen playing chess in the Café Central, *far right*. Trieste's old-fashioned Caffe San Marco has not changed in 100 years. In Vienna, Adolf Loos's Café Museum on the Karlsplatz, the Hawelka (favored by the intellectuals), and the charming Pruckl are coming back into fashion. So too is Budapest's Hungaria, *right*, formerly called the Café New York, which was the center of the city's literary life until the 1930s.

Café Sperl was one of Vienna's most famous coffeehouses. Founded in 1880, it still has much of its original decor, including its Thonet chairs, its billiard tables, and its ocher-colored walls, which have become even more patinated with years of cigarette smoke.

Between Two Wars

The formation of the Republic of Austria in 1919 brought the beginnings of public housing to Vienna. One of the most famous building complexes of the socialist movement of the 1920s is the gigantic Karl-Marx-Hof complex. Over two miles long and including 1,600 units, it was built by Karl Ehn in 1927. The

fortresslike building, with its red and ocher cement exterior, was one of the main sites of the sociodemocratic resistance against fascism during the Austrian Civil War in 1934.

Between 1920 and 1938, the functionalist school produced a few isolated and remarkable works in Vienna, including the house that the philosopher Ludwig Wittgenstein designed for his sister Gretl with the architect Paul Engelmann in 1926. Reflecting the strictness of the principles of Adolf Loos, the house—with its stark minimalist facade, its total lack of ornamentation, and its beautifully proportioned spaces—is a stylistic exercise of the highest order. It is also an intellectual manifesto in which philosopher and architect worked together in perfect accord.

ABOVE *The bell panel in the lobby is typical of many turn-of-the-century Viennese apartment buildings.*

ABOVE RIGHT *Praun has placed two Thonet armchairs and the prototype of a secretary she recently designed for a yacht in the foyer.*

RIGHT *One of Praun's chair designs is by the door of the study. Bronze sculptures by Bertoni Wander and Maria Bilger stand on a Biedermeier chest. The charcoal drawing on the wall is by Clarice Praun, an artist and relative.*

FAR RIGHT *The furniture in the living room is an eclectic mix of modern and Biedermeier pieces. Praun designed the sofa for the noted conductor Herbert von Karajan. The reinterpretation of the Windsor chair is a 1930s piece by Josef Frank, who designed the Wiedenhofer-Hof housing complex in Vienna.*

An Architect's Selective Eye

Anna-Lülja Praun, a Russian architect, has lived in the same apartment in Vienna for more than 60 years. She has furnished the rooms with both her own furniture designs and a personal collection of pieces that have come to be synonymous with design in the early 20th century.

Praun's personality, as well as her memories, offer a link to a world of which few images are left. Throughout, there is never the sense of being in an apartment that belongs to an elderly person. On the contrary, Praun has developed her own sense of minimalism. She has not kept every bibelot or knickknack. Her selective eye bears witness to an unusual sensibility and rigorousness that still, and maybe even more today, can be described as modern.

TOP *A gouache by Sonia Delaunay has been hung between a photograph Delaunay inscribed to her friend "Lull" Praun and a photograph of the architect with Eileen Gray, taken in Paris in the late 1960s.*

ABOVE *On the plan file in the study, Praun has placed a ceramic piece by Franz-Josef Altenburg, sculptures by Walter Ritter, a portrait of Wassily Kandinsky, and a study for a pink Wiener Werkstätte textile by Josef Hoffmann.*

RIGHT *Praun's lifelong passion for bentwood chairs is evident in the collection that surrounds the bookcases in her study.*

In 1903, the Municipality of Prague decided to offer the city a building where civic and cultural affairs could take place. The result, designed by Antonin Balsanek and Osvald Polivka, was an imposing structure that represents a high point of art nouveau architecture as influenced by Viennese Secessionism.

The monumental entrance on Republic Square is topped by a dome whose front is decorated with an allegorical mosaic by Karel Spillar, *left.*

The interior decorations, including the ones in the large restaurant that forms part of the complex, *right,* were undertaken by such artists as Mikolas Ales, Emanuel Novak, and Ladislav Saloun, who belonged to the Czech School at the beginning of the century. The most famous contributor was Alphonse Maria Mucha.

Municipal Cultural Center

The Municipal Building complex also includes the Smetana Concert Hall, a spacious restaurant, a café, and a bar. These rooms offer examples of all the crafts of the Jugendstil—especially metalwork and stained glass.

ABOVE AND OPPOSITE *After Mucha's return to Bohemia from Paris, his first important commission was the decoration of the Mayor's Room in the Prague Municipal Building, where he created a series of controversial symbolist murals.*

SZENTENDRE

Artists' Eclectic Choices

Szentendre, or St. Andrew, a small old town located about 12 miles outside Budapest on the western bank of the Danube, has in the last few decades become a place where artists and writers particularly chose to live.

It was in the 18th century that Szentendre flourished, and there are many buildings and squares that still recall the atmosphere of the Dalmatian-Baroque towns of the period.

Two painters, husband and wife, have settled in one of the town's small houses, which they have restored themselves. Enthusiastic travelers, they have a taste for the unusual and have filled the rooms with enviable collections of musical instruments, primitive portraits, and religious porcelains, many of which they have gleaned from the Budapest flea market and in the antiques shops that have cropped up only in the last few years.

ABOVE *A carved wood cherub hangs in the living room. The hanging shelves are crammed with porcelain figurines.*

RIGHT *A wood virgin and child stands in front of a bookcase that was once part of the built-in furniture in an old apothecary shop.*

216

LEFT *A group of 19th-century lithographs hang above a Thonet bentwood office chair in the hall.*

TOP AND ABOVE *Two vintage stoves—one a Victorian cast-iron model, the other a traditional ceramic—are used to heat the studio and the living room, respectively.*

Religious porcelain statuettes crowd the shelves in the studio. Small china holy-water fonts complete the collection.

The painted banquette, traditional pottery, brightly hued woven tablecloth, and the series of 19th-century primitive portraits give the dining area its Hungarian folk art—influenced style.

Knickknacks are lined up on the shelves of the apothecary shop fittings. The chest drawers that once held medicinal herbs have enamel labels written in Latin and some of the original colored-glass knobs.

The glass-fronted store fitting in the living room is filled with violins and clarinets, part of the collection of musical instruments.

Dolls—of cloth, paper, and celluloid—of all sizes are the theme of another collection that is housed in the studio.

Old tools, including a variety of files and rasps, are displayed in a wood rack.

DER · ZEIT · IHRE · KVNST·
DER · KVNST · IHRE · FREIHEIT·

SACRVM·

Two Secession
Masterworks

Vienna's Secession Building, *opposite*, Joseph Maria Olbrich's 1897 masterpiece, was the architectural statement of the Secession movement. With its dome of gilded and interwoven laurel leaves and its shiny white walls, the building was a symbol of antiacademicism. The family of owls is one of many decorative motifs on the exterior. Among the inscriptions that appear on the building is the motto *Der Zeit Ihre Kunst; Der Kunst Ihre Freiheit*, or "To each time its art; to art its freedom."

Otto Wagner's 1906 Kaiserbad lockhouse, *right*, on the left bank of the canal of the Danube in Vienna, is one of the architect's most charming late works. Even though the lock was never installed, the building, with its granite base, copper roof, and marble-bolted walls, was one of the great architect's most innovative designs. The decorative frieze of blue ceramic tiles that edges the facade evokes the movement of the waves.

In the Spirit of Vienna

In Budapest in 1905, a Hungarian architect whose name is now lost to us designed a grand family house in the Vienna Secession manner for a wealthy German banker.

Today, all that remains from the house on the hill that overlooks the Danube is its ground floor. Carefully protected and transformed into an apartment, it is one of the rare interiors still intact from the modernist period in Budapest. The geometric motifs and ornamentation give the rooms an overall feeling of severity. This is in keeping with the spirit of the Wiener Werkstätte, the design movement that was so appreciated by the forward-thinking people of the day.

Some of the design details that have survived include the geometric wood stair balustrade and the mosaic-tile table. Once one of the numerous reception rooms, the living room is still furnished with its original pieces by Josef Hoffmann, which include a table, chairs, and settee. In contrast, the patinated hammered-metal front door with its raised plaque engraved with the name Jozsef Somlo shows the ravages that many such buildings have suffered since they were first built at the beginning of the century.

JOSEF
HOFFMANN

Attention to Details

Located in a mountainous region of lower Austria, near Hohenberg, this country house is surrounded by a forest of evergreens. Called Bergerhohe, it belonged to Paul Wittgenstein, an uncle of the philosopher Ludwig Wittgenstein and a member of one of the wealthiest and most influential families in Austria. In 1899, Josef Hoffmann, already well known as a leader of the Viennese avant-garde, was commissioned to renovate the rustic house.

The project was to become one of the 29-year-old architect's most important early works. Influenced by the English Arts and Crafts movement, Hoffmann's interior was designed for every detail to be carried out by craftsmen working together to create a unified whole. The house is not only Hoffmann's interpretation of a rusticated style but heralds the beginnings of the Viennese Jugendstil, which would revolutionize the world of European art and design.

OPPOSITE, LEFT, AND ABOVE *When Josef Hoffmann reworked the exterior of the traditional farm in lower Austria, he had a verse by Martin Luther inscribed over the front porch:* Das Haus des Friedes in Stille, *or "The House of Peace in Stillness."*

227

LEFT *The living room has been executed with oak paneling in the Arts and Crafts style. Many furnishings, including the coat-rack, side tables, and window seat, have been built in.*

ABOVE *The grid of small square panes of glass on the door from the bedroom to the bath is an early example of what was to become one of Hoffmann's favorite motifs.*

Art nouveau pottery stands in a niche cabinet built into the arch that separates the living room from the alcoved bedroom.

Hoffmann designed all the details, including the wall stencils, woodwork, and brass hardware.

The brass table lamp is also a Hoffmann design. The alcove bed is an example of the designer's integration of furniture and architecture.

In a corner of the bedroom, a wicker chair stands near the wardrobe, also a Hoffmann design.

Hoffmann topped the door that leads from the living room to the hall with a graphic version of Paul Wittgenstein's initials.

The rustic wood staircase, stained in red, has been decorated with an art nouveau pattern of stylized flowers.

On the landing, small glass panes are set
into a wood grid, behind which the
laundry has been installed.

The enclosed veranda of rough-hewn wood, located off the master bedroom, acts as a transition between the forest and the interior.

The master bedroom has been furnished in a rather rudimentary way, reflecting the idea its occupants had of the simple life in the country.

The bathroom, with its tiled and sunken bathtub, was inspired by the spas that were fashionable at the time.

Collections of antlers line the walls of the landing and second-floor sitting room. The sitting room was furnished by Wittgenstein's descendants in a Biedermeier style that has little do to with Hoffmann—testimony to the fact that it was not until the sixties that people started to recognize and appreciate the importance of Hoffmann's design.

Czech Cubism

I n the first two decades of the century, Czech cubism became the synthesis of modernism in architecture. It was the culmination of Bohemia's architectural heritage, combining the Baroque style, with its bold chiaroscuro effects, and the Secession, with its emphasis on geometric and abstract details. Prague was the only city in the world where the theories of the French cubist movement—especially the ideas in the paintings of Pablo Picasso and Georges Braque—were translated into three-dimensional architecture.

The exceptional character of cubist architecture led to an explosion of form, with building surfaces deconstructed in sharply angled facets as in Josef Chochol's apartment building, *above far left*, which dates from 1912, *above left*. The large apartment building complex designed by Otakar Novotny in 1917, *below far left*, illustrates a series of architectonic variations on the triangle and is one of the most startling examples of cubist architecture in Prague. Josef Gocar's 1912 apartment building, *left*, is known as the House of the Black Virgin and is also considered a masterpiece of the style.

From 1920 to 1925, the angular and prismatic shapes of the early buildings were replaced by softer and more cylindrical forms that became known as part of the rondocubist movement, *right*.

The angular, sharp-edged forms of Czech cubism were also interpreted in objects, such as this prismatic clock.

1683   1939

CUTTINGS FROM THE MITTEL EUROPA
Gazette

Wien

Last week The Blue Bottle, a coffee-house, opened for business in Vienna. Patrons were encouraged to linger and talk. Proprietor Kolschitsky serves the bitter Turkish brew with sugar and cream.

Hapsburg Versailles

Leading figure of Baroque architecture Johann Bernhard Fischer von Erlach has completed his design for the new Hapsburg residence. Castle Schönbrunn will be built outside of Vienna.

Schloss Schönbrunn proposal 1694

Johann Christian Gunther, German poet (Poeta Laureatus)

Death Notices

Johann Bernhard Fischer von Erlach,

Court Architect, died in his 67th year. He was responsible for designing the Karlskirche in Vienna, The Church of Holy Trinity in Salzburg, and The Clam-Gallas Palace in Prague. His most recent building, The National Library in Vienna, will be completed by his son, Joseph Emmanuel.

Birth Announcements

Johann Bernhard Hagedorn

Porcelain to be manufactured in Vienna

Just two years ago Johann Friedrich Böttger standardized the manufacture of porcelain in Meissen, Saxony. In a few days the kilns in Vienna's new porcelain factory will be fired, the forms will be poured, and Vienna will begin producing porcelain of its own.

PROTESTANTS EXPELLED

29. MAY. 1731

SALZBURG

An estimated 12,000 Protestants were expelled from their homes in Salzburg last week. King Frederick William of Prussia has announced his plans to allow the exiled Protestants to settle in Eastern Prussia without monetary penalty.

1751

Fashion News

The minuet stands unrivaled. In ballrooms and dance halls all across Europe people are dancing the minuet, and nothing but the minuet.

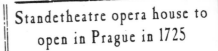

Standetheatre opera house to open in Prague in 1725

1754

GHETTO FIRE

PRAGUE -

A FIRE THAT HAS RAGED THROUGH THE JEWISH GHETTO IN PRAGUE HAS BEEN EXTINGUISHED. AMONG THE BUILDINGS IT DESTROYED ARE THE OLD MAISEL GYPSY AND HIGH COURT SYNAGOGUES, THE JEWISH TOWN HALL, THE HOSPITAL, AND THE ORPHANAGE. WITNESSES SAID

Birth Announcement November 2, 1755
Marie Antoinette Josephe Johanna, born to Maria Theresa and Francis I.

Ablegati Turchi, born to Francesca and Garibaldi

Haydn appointed Kapellmeister

(1761)

Austrian composer Franz Josef Haydn was appointed Kapellmeister to the Esterházy Court of Hungary.

THE ARTS 1791

Mozart's *Magic Flute* Debuts

Mozart's new opera, *The Magic Flute* (with libretto by Schikaneder) premiered at theater An der Wien last night. Critics were less than enthusiastic,

1792
Promising Composer Comes to Vienna

A young man by the name of Ludwig van Beethoven arrived in Vienna from Bonn last month. He has established himself in Prince Lichnowsky's household and is studying under Haydn, Albrechtsberger, and Salieri. The latter two report Beethoven to possess an unusual degree of talent. Vienna can expect to hear more from him in the future.

DEATH NOTICES 1809

May 31, Vienna, Franz Josef Haydn.
The retired composer for the Esterházy family has died at 77 years of age. His musical service in the Esterházy Court, "with no one about to confuse and torment" him, allowed Haydn to develop in a truly original direction.

METTERNICH TO BE APPOINTED AUSTRIAN FOREIGN MINISTER

(1809)

1762
Prodigies play at Schönbrunn

A six-year-old musician, Wolfgang Amadeus Mozart, and his nine-year-old sister, 'Nannerl,' made their debut performance at Schönbrunn Castle. The empress and her family, including seven-year-old Marie Antoinette, enjoyed the performance. Afterward young Wolfgang made a seat of the empress's lap. Leopold Mozart, father of the two musicians, revealed plans to begin a musical tour through Europe with them in the coming year.

results have been somewhat successful.
On an experimental front, Austrian physician Friedrich Anton Mesmer has been using hypnosis on his patients to assist in curing their ailments. *1774*

1783 RELIGIOUS TOLERANCE GRANTED

Emperor Joseph II has granted the long-disputed Patent of Religious Tolerance toward Lutherans, Calvinists, and the Greek Orthodox. Pope Pius VI's pleas to rescind his policy of tolerance have so far gone unheeded.

Birth Announcements 1791
Vienna, January 15
Franz Grillparzer, born to Wenzel Grillparzer, lawyer

1808
Fashion Notes

This season pigtails for men have become decidedly unfashionable, and one now sees shorter hairstyles of more uniform length accented by prominent sideburns.

1820
MUSIC TO DANCE TO

Composers Josef Lanner and Johann Strauss fill Viennese dance halls with music in three-quarter time. These compositions, designed especially for the waltz, satisfy the dancers' desire to twirl on the downbeat.

VIENNA 1825

Building of synagogues in Vienna is legalized

HALLEY'S COMET RETURNS

1835 NEWS SUMMARY ON PAGE 8

1827 Vienna mourns the death of composer Ludwig van Beethoven in his 56th year.

DEATHS
November 19, 1829

Vienna: Franz Peter Schubert, composer, died of typhus. At his request his body will be buried near Beethoven's grave. Dramatist Franz Grillparzer has written for his epitaph, "Music has here buried a rich treasure but even lovelier hopes."

◄◊§§◊► ◄◊§§◊► ◄◊§§◊► ✿ ◄◊§§◊► ◄◊§§◊►
*Birth announcement 13 July 1841
Vienna, Otto Wagner: born to Rudolf
Simeon and Susanne Wagner*
◄◊§§◊► ◄◊§§◊► ◄◊§§◊► ✿ ◄◊§§◊► ◄◊§§◊►

THE VIENNA THEATER 1833

Der böse Geist lumpazivagabundus,
Johann Nestroy's satirical play, will be performed for the 75th time this year. Two more performances are scheduled before the year's end.

Tickets are available from

HUNGARIAN ACADEMY OF SCIENCES TO OPEN IN 1825

MAY 1839

Liszt Visits Hungary

On his tour through Europe composer Franz Liszt visited Hungary for the first time since his boyhood. He was influenced by the Gypsy music that he heard

PRAGUE 1845

Central Train Station Completed

The inaugural train will arrive at Central Station tomorrow afternoon. Regular service begins early next week.

PRAGUE STREETS LIT BY GAS LAMPS

VIENNA

Working under harsh censorship from Franz I, Viennese dramatist Franz Grillparzer has continued to write. His new novella, The Poor Fiddler, *will be available for purchase later this month.*

1853: A RAILROAD OPENS THROUGH THE ALPS

The new Semmerling Railroad line connecting Trieste to Vienna completed its first successful voyage yesterday. Employing new tunneling and switchback methods, it is the first railroad to cut through the Alps, drastically cutting traveling time while allowing passengers to enjoy a breathtaking view of the mountains.

DEATHS
July 31, 1849

Hungary: Sandor Petöfi, Magyar nationalist poet, was killed at the age of 27 years while fighting in the battle of Segesvar.

September 1, 1864

LIBERAL NEWSPAPER PUBLISHED

The *Neue Freie Presse* released its first edition today. Copies were circulated throughout the city and customers were

---

March 3, 1848

Kossuth Speaks Out

Hungarian nationalist Lajos Kossuth has condemned Austrian policies toward Hungary and demanded that Metternich be removed from office.

CHURCH PLANNED FOR RINGSTRASSE

VIENNA 1858

Several months ago Franz Josef ordered the old fortification surrounding inner Vienna to be converted for civilian use. The Votivkirche, designed by architect Heinrich von Ferstel, will be the first new building constructed on the site.

Illustrierte Zeitun

MARCH 15, 1848

REVOLT IN THE EMPIRE

General unrest in the empire has turned into revolt. Yesterday, a stirring speech by Dr. Adolf Fischoff was enough to send Viennese protesters pouring into the streets. Printers, citizens, and students stormed the House of Deputies, demanding civil rights and the removal of the hated chancellor Metternich. The emperor chose to suppress the revolt and 45 protesters were killed. A similar Czech uprising was suppressed by Austrian troops under Windischgratz. Metternich was seen fleeing Vienna in disguise by night.

MARCH 15, 1848

JEWS OF BOHEMIA AND MORAVIA EMANCIPATED

March 15, 1848

Censorship lifted. Viennese granted free press

ARTS 1866

BARTERED BRIDE PREMIERE

Last night Bedrich Smetana, conductor of the National Theater in Prague, introduced Czech modern music to the world with his opera *The Bartered Bride.*

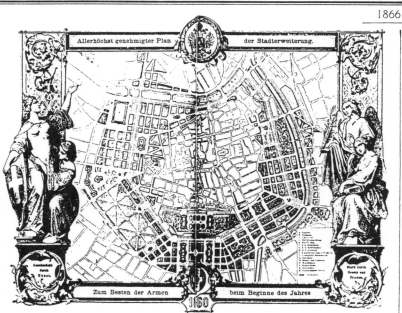

1866

Allerhöchst genehmigter Plan   der Stadterweiterung.

Zum Besten der Armen   beim Beginne des Jahres

1160

Building the Ringstrasse

The old fortification that encircled inner Vienna is slowly being replaced by a large public boulevard. Situated around the ring will be a number of buildings, each based on revered architectural styles of the past. Plans for the town hall are late Gothic Flemish, the art museum will be rusticated Italian, and the opera house is a large version of Renaissance design. No costs will be spared for materials or construction of the Ringstrasse.

JUNE 1873 WORLD'S FAIR REPORT

CHOLERA AFFECTS ATTENDANCE

The World's Fair opened in the Prater last month, but with cholera gripping the city of Vienna, attendance at the fair has remained very low. Various presses have avoided reporting on the severity of the epidemic in hopes of encouraging international attendance.

VIENNA : CITY REPORT

CITY-RUN HOSPITAL OPENS

1873 : Vienna's first city-run hospital is open. Until now the duty of running hospitals has belonged to the church. Now in the name of science, the state will assume some of that responsibility.

Births	1875

Prague, 4 December
Rainer Maria Rilke
born to Josef Rilke and

JUNE 5, 1883

ORIENT EXPRESS

Surrounded by cheers and waving arms, three coaches of the Orient Express railroad departed Paris early today on its inaugural voyage. The train will pass through Vienna and Budapest before reaching its final destination of Bucharest. The trip is expected to take about 80 hours to complete.

Bedrich Smetana, *1884*
with financial support from **Liszt,** to open music school in Prague. (see full story p. 15)

"BLUE DANUBE" WALTZ COMES TO VIENNA

Johann Strauss the younger gained critics' praise when his "Blue Danube" waltz premiered at the Paris Exhibition. Tomorrow evening "Blue Danube" will be performed here in Vienna for the first time.

Opera house opening is overshadowed

VIENNA 1868

When the Opera house on the Ringstrasse was completed, Emperor Franz Joseph was overheard to say that the facade of the building appeared too low. The building's facade was, in fact, lower than in the architect's plan because during the construction of the building, the street level was unexpectedly raised a meter or so. In response to the emperor's criticism the building's architect, Eduard van der Nüll, hanged himself. As a result Emperor Franz Joseph is refusing to make his aesthetic opinions public, offering only, when he is pressed, "It was very beautiful, I enjoyed it

---

Education Reforms Passed

Primary schooling is now compulsory for the children of Vienna. The new laws will be effect

---

1873

Buda and Pest unite to form Hungary's capital

THE ARTS 1888
Burghtheater's last performance

The cream of Vienna's society showed up to witness the last performance held at the Burghtheater. The theater had served as a stage for both new and revered artists from all over Europe since its opening in 1741. Mozart's Marriage of Figaro debuted there in 1786. At the end of tonight's performance theatergoers rushed the stage and tore it down. Many leaving the building were seen holding splinters from the stage and shreds of curtains to preserve as keepsakes of the era.

1891

Electrically powered trams replace horse trams in Prague

1893
SCHNITZLER'S ANATOL

The new work, a cycle of one-act plays with characters overlapping from one play to the next, is a social critique played out against an easy-going Viennese background.

1895: New Publications

Otto Wagner publishes *Modern Architecture*.

GUSTAV KLIMT COMMISSIONED

1893

The Austrian minister of culture decided yesterday on commissioning Gustav Klimt to create the paintings for the ceiling of the university's great lecture hall. Klimt is one of the artists responsible for the ceiling frescoes in the staircases of the Burghtheater. The works planned for the lecture hall will symbolize the disciplines of the school: philosophy, jurisprudence, and medicine.

1894 sees a new style from Alphonse Mucha

Graphic designer Alphonse Maria Mucha has designed a theater poster of Sarah Bernhardt as Victorien Sardou's *Gismonda*. Composed of sleek lines and arabesque flourishes, the poster announces the spread of the style "Art Nouveau," or "Style Mucha."

Several young artists and architects have formed a group called the Vienna Secession, whose aim is to blaze the trail for the future of Viennese art. Founding members of the group include Joseph Maria Olbrich, Koloman Moser, and Josef Hoffmann, with painter Gustav Klimt as president. As a new master of the "old school," Klimt was a natural choice for the position. (1897)

SACHERTORTE BATTLE ENDS

A seven-year court case on the rights of the recipe for Sachertorte was finally decided in favor of Hotel Sacher. Demel's Pastry Shop and Hotel Sacher have long been battling over rights of ownership of the chocolate pastry. Demel's claims that the layer of fruit rests on top of the pastry. Hotel Sacher maintains that the layer of fruit goes in the middle. Henceforth, only the original pastry may be called "Sachertorte," and all others must use the name "Sacher torte."

1898

SECESSIONIST PAVILION COMPLETE

The Secessionist Pavilion, designed by Joseph Maria Olbrich, opens Tuesday. The facade consists of smooth, undecorated planes, and the simple construction is topped with an intricate openwork dome of laurel leaves. The interior space is divided by movable partitions upon which artworks will be displayed. The concept of a changeable display space is in keeping with Secessionist belief that uncertainty and flexibility are essential to the growth of art. The epigraph above the main entrance, "To each age its art/to art its freedom," could also serve as a motto of the Secessionist movement in general.

1896

Prague Ghetto to Be Torn Down

Over 50 years ago the Prague Jewish ghetto was officially absorbed by the city under the name "Josefstadt." The buildings comprising that area are now charted to be pulled down for reasons stated as "hygienic." Historic buildings, such as Town Hall, and the Maisel and Hoch synagogues will be spared. The historic Josefov cemetery will also remain.

VER·SACRVM

ORGAN·DER·VEREINIGUNG·BILDENDER·KVENSTLER·ÖSTERREICHS·

JANUAR ·1898·

JAEHRLICH·12·HEFTE IM·ABONNEMENT·6·FL·:OM

New Publications for 1898

The first issue of the square-format Secessionist magazine, Ver Sacrum, was released. The periodical will publish artwork, architectural plans, and writings of the Secessionists. Depicted on the front cover of the first issue is

"The Interpretation of Dreams"

Sigmund Freud's new publication is due out next year.

1900

THE POSTAL SAVINGS BANK BUILDING OPENS

1906.

Architect Otto Wagner has reached new levels of refinement with his design for the Postal Savings Bank. Plain marble slabs anchored to the understructure by aluminum bolts create a facade that is at once lean and rich. The Postal Savings Bank was created as a state-supported agency for smaller investors to pool their funds in an effort to offset the power of the wealthy few in the "Rothschild Party."

Mahler dedicates his "Symphony of a Thousand"

407

Composer Gustav Mahler is now on his way to the United States, but before departing he dedicated his newest symphony to his wife. Like much of Mahler's work, Symphony of a Thousand (so-called because it requires hundreds of players for its execution) achieves a balance between dynamic lyricism and a modern romanticism.

1908 ILLUSTRIERTE ZEITUNG

PSYCHOANALYTIC SOCIETY OF VIENNA

Sigmund Freud has founded a group dedicated to furthering study in the relatively new science of psychology. Its

---

1902

Art Exhibitions

An exhibition of work by French sculptor

Auguste Rodin

opens in Prague.

1905

NOBEL PEACE PRIZE

Viennese pacifist and novelist

Bertha von Suttner

made history this week as the first woman to win a Nobel Prize. In 1889, Suttner published her anti-war novel, *Lay Down Your Arms*. Throughout her life she has dedicated herself to peace efforts.

WIENER WERKSTÄTTE MOVEMENT FORMED

This 1903 offspring of the Secessionist movement was created by Koloman Moser and Josef Hoffmann, with financial assistance by Fritz Waerndorfer. The company is dedicated to producing crafts of an artistic nature to further close the gap between fine and applied art. The Werkstätte was inspired by a similar group established by William Morris and Charles Robert Ashbee in England.

1905

Exhibitions in Prague

Norwegian painter Edvard Munch shows his paintings this week (see review p. 14B)

A "House Without Eyebrows" for 1910

A commercial building on the Michaelerplatz, designed by Adolf Loos, has been completed. Typical of Loos's designs, the facade of the new building is not embellished with decoration. The windows, set nearly flush with the outer walls, have no sills and are uniform in size and treatment. The emperor, whose favorite windows overlook the new building, is dismayed by its starkness and is keeping the shutters closed to block the view.

DER NEUE RAUM

1911

CUBIST ARTISTS FORM GROUP IN PRAGUE

Artists Vincenc Benes, Emil Filla, Otto Guttfreund, Václav Spála, and Joseph Capek found the group Cubist Plastic Artists in the interest of Czech cubism.

1912

NEW ART: VIENNA

Oskar Kokoschka reports he is nearly finished painting a series he calls "Neurotic Portraits."

Painter Egon Schiele Jailed

Schiele is charged with "disseminating obscene drawings," and sentenced to three days imprisonment in St. Pölen. After the trial the ruling judge publicly burned one of the drawings.

June 28, 1914

FRANZ FERDINAND AND SOPHIE ASSASSINATED

Heir to the Hapsburg throne Archduke Franz Ferdinand and Archduchess Sophie were assassinated in Sarajevo by Bosnian nationalist Gavrilo Princip. The murders have fueled existing tensions in the region.

Egon Schiele †

October 31, 1918. Viennese painter Egon Schiele has died of Spanish influenza just six months after his paintings began to meet with success in Vienna.

July 28, 1914
NEWS IN BRIEF

Austria declares war on Serbia

The Great War Begins

Trieste promised to Italy:1915

In a secret treaty, the Allies promised to return the city of Trieste and other territories of *Italia Irredenta* to Italy after their intended victory in the war.

MA GROUP BANNED

KASSÁK IMPRISONED

1 9 1 6

Less than one year ago, artist Lajos Kassák formed an activist artist group called MA and began to publish the group's eponymous magazine. MA considered artistic revolution and political/social change to be inseparably linked. With the fall of the Hungarian Socialist Republic the activist magazine, which was seen as a threat, was banned and its founder imprisoned.

VIENNA, NOVEMBER 21, 1916

Austria sees the end of an era as the last of the Hapsburg emperors, Franz Joseph, dies at Schönbrunn, outside Vienna. He was 86.

ARTS REVIEW 1919

Alphonse Maria Mucha is to design the first banknotes and stamps for the new Czechoslovakia. The com

New Exhibitions
December 1923

Arranged by the Czech artists group Devetsil, "The Bazaar of Modern Arts" opened at the House of Artists in Prague. On display are such "Dadaist" objects as a set of ball bearings, a mirror, and a hairdresser's dummy, complete with wig, entitled "Modern Sculpture." More traditional drawings and paintings are also on display. The show is a celebration of the modern and utilitarian. The exhibit is scheduled to move to Brno in early 1924.

Wiener Werkstätte dissolves 1932

Sept. 1, 1939

NEWS REVIEW

German Troops Invade Poland

World War II Begins

28 *October*, 1918 WORLD NEWS

Czechoslovakia claims its independence

Tomás Garrigue Masaryk has been named president of the new state. Prague is officially declared the capital.

INDEX

STYLE LIBRARY

French Style
BY SUZANNE SLESIN & STAFFORD CLIFF
PHOTOGRAPHS BY JACQUES DIRAND

The innovative and trendsetting series of all-color books that focuses on and celebrates design and decorating in different countries. Private homes and public buildings, gardens, and city and country landscapes have offered inspirational glimpses into a diversity of cultures and lifestyles that continue to excite and capture our interest.

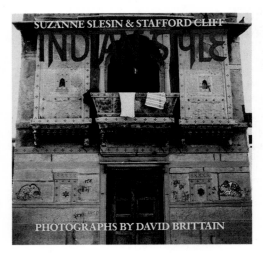

SUZANNE SLESIN & STAFFORD CLIFF
INDIAN STYLE
PHOTOGRAPHS BY DAVID BRITTAIN

SUZANNE SLESIN & STAFFORD CLIFF · PHOTOGRAPHS BY KEN KIRKWOOD
English Style

CARIBBEAN STYLE
BY SUZANNE SLESIN & STAFFORD CLIFF
JACK BERTHELOT, MARTINE GAUMÉ, DANIEL ROZENSZTROCH
PHOTOGRAPHS BY GILLES DE CHABANEIX
FOREWORD BY JAN MORRIS

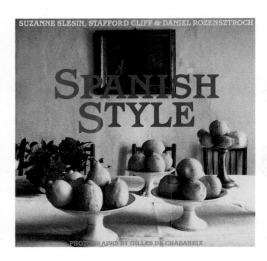

SUZANNE SLESIN, STAFFORD CLIFF & DANIEL ROZENSZTROCH
SPANISH STYLE
PHOTOGRAPHS BY GILLES DE CHABANEIX

SUZANNE SLESIN, STAFFORD CLIFF & DANIEL ROZENSZTROCH
JAPANESE STYLE
PHOTOGRAPHS BY GILLES DE CHABANEIX

SUZANNE SLESIN, STAFFORD CLIFF & DANIEL ROZENSZTROCH
Greek Style
PHOTOGRAPHS BY GILLES DE CHABANEIX

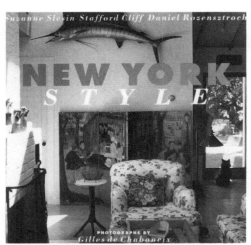

Suzanne Slesin Stafford Cliff Daniel Rozensztroch
NEW YORK STYLE
PHOTOGRAPHS BY
Gilles de Chabaneix

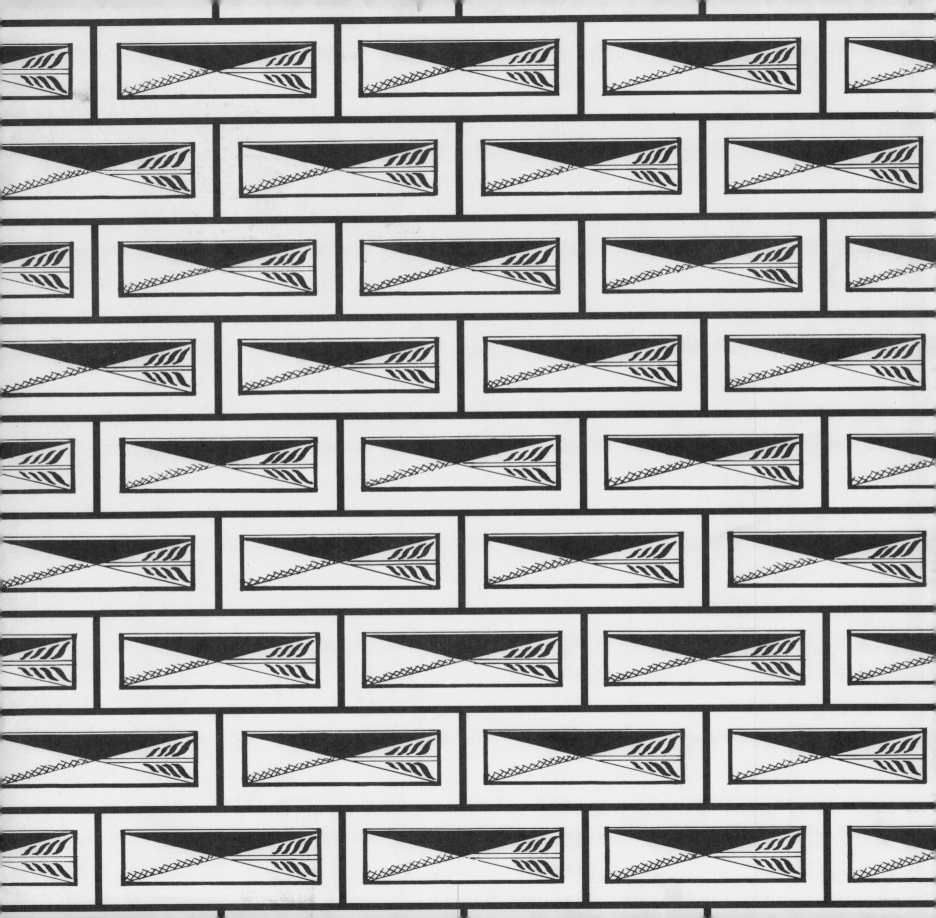